easy
curries

easy curries

100 fuss-free recipes for everyday cooking

M&S

Marks and Spencer plc
PO Box 3339
Chester CH99 9QS

shop online

www.marksandspencer.com

ISBN: 978-1-84960-747-6

Printed in China

Introduction by Linda Doeser
New recipes by Sandra Baddeley
Cover photography by Clive Streeter
Additional photography by Mike Cooper
Cover food styling by Teresa Goldfinch
Additional food styling by Sumi Glass

The views expressed in this book are those of the author but they are general views only and readers are urged to consult a relevant and qualified specialist for individual advice in particular situations. Marks and Spencer plc and Exclusive Editions Publishing Ltd hereby exclude all liability to the extent permitted by law for any errors or omissions in this book and for any loss, damage or expense (whether direct or indirect) suffered by a third party relying on any information contained in this book.

Notes for the Reader
This book uses both metric and imperial measurements. Follow the same units of measurement throughout; do not mix metric and imperial. All spoon measurements are level: teaspoons are assumed to be 5 ml, and tablespoons are assumed to be 15 ml. Unless otherwise stated, milk is assumed to be full fat, eggs and individual vegetables are medium, and pepper is freshly ground black pepper. Unless otherwise stated, all root vegetables should be washed and peeled prior to using.

Garnishes, decorations and serving suggestions are all optional and not necessarily included in the recipe ingredients or method.

The times given are an approximate guide only. Preparation times differ according to the techniques used by different people and the cooking times may also vary from those given. Optional ingredients, variations or serving suggestions have not been included in the time calculations.

Recipes using raw or very lightly cooked eggs should be avoided by infants, the elderly, pregnant women, convalescents and anyone suffering from an illness. Pregnant and breastfeeding women are advised to avoid eating peanuts and peanut products. Sufferers from nut allergies should be aware that some of the ready-made ingredients used in the recipes in this book may contain nuts. Always check the packaging before use.

Vegetarians should be aware that some of the ready-made ingredients used in the recipes in this book may contain animal products. Always check the packaging before use.

For front cover recipe, please see page 44

Contents

Introduction

The word curry comes from the Tamil word, kari, which simply means sauce – something of a modest understatement as a description of this most popular and versatile of dishes. Curries are associated with both the countries of the Indian sub-continent, such as India, Pakistan and Sri Lanka, and the countries of South-east Asia, such as Thailand, but curries are now a popular choice in many homes and restaurants worldwide.

There is a widespread belief that making an authentic curry is a difficult and time-consuming process but nothing could be further from the truth. Whether based on meat, poultry, fish, seafood or vegetables, they are nearly all straightforward one-pot dishes. The secret of a curry's success lies in the imaginative and subtle use of spices and other flavourings. Chillies, whether fresh, dried or powdered, give the dishes heat in varying degrees, but that is only part of the story. Fragrant spices, such as coriander, fennel seeds and saffron, provide aroma. Sweet or sour spices, such as cinnamon and nutmeg or tamarind and turmeric, offer a complex contrast of flavours. Pungent spices, such as fenugreek and mustard seeds, give depth to a dish, while fresh spices, such as ginger and lemon grass, add a refreshing sharpness.

Nowadays, most supermarkets stock a wide range of such spices as well as other authentic ingredients for curries, such as Thai fish sauce, kaffir lime leaves, curry leaves, fresh coriander, canned coconut milk and all kinds of dahl. There are also some excellent brands of ready-made Thai curry pastes and the Indian spice mix garam masala available if you don't have the time or confidence to make them yourself. The other ingredients used in curries will be familiar, everyday items – vegetables such as tomatoes, peppers and onions, meat and fish, lemons and limes, vegetable oil, yogurt and herbs such as bay leaves and mint.

It should be clear that while curries are always full of spice, they are not necessarily mouth-searingly hot – although some are definitely not for the faint-hearted! There are dishes to suit all tastes from a cool, creamy korma to a scorching vindaloo and from aromatic prawns in coconut milk to the pungent do piaza with its characteristic two types of onion. Of course, when serving curry, the right accompaniments add to the sheer pleasure of the meal. The final chapter in this book not only provides recipes for flavoursome rice, but also breads, pickles and side dishes.

Top Tips for Success

• Dried spices quickly lose their flavour and aroma so it is best to buy them in small quantities. While they look decorative on a wall rack in the kitchen, it is better to store them in airtight containers in a cool dark place. Replace them every six months.

• Whole spices and seeds keep better than round spices and recipes often require spices to be roasted or dry-fried whole and then ground, crushed or puréed into a paste. You can use a pestle and mortar, a spice mill or even an electric coffee grinder kept specifically for the purpose.

• It is difficult to tell how hot chillies are just by looking at them. As a general rule, small pointed chillies are hotter than larger round ones, but there are exceptions. Even chillies from the same bush may vary in the intensity of their heat. Green (unripe) chillies are hotter than red.

• The heat of chillies is concentrated in the membranes, so removing the seeds reduces the heat. Cut the chilli in half lengthways, then use a small sharp knife to scrape out the seeds and fleshy white membranes. You can then slice or dice them as required. Always wash your hands thoroughly after handling chillies and be careful

not to touch sensitive areas of your skin, such as the eyes or mouth. If your skin is very sensitive, wear latex or plastic gloves or de-seed and chop chillies using a knife and fork.

• To prepare fresh ginger, peel off the skin with a paring knife, then put the root on a chopping board and crush lightly with the flat blade of a cook's knife. Chop or shred according to the recipe.

• To prepare lemon grass, cut off the dry tops to leave about 15 cm/6 inches of stalk. Peel off the coarse outer layers. Put the stalk on a chopping board, place the flat side of a heavy cook's knife on top and hit it with your fist to bruise, then slice thinly and chop finely.

• Note that there is a difference between coconut milk sold in cans and the thin, pale liquid found inside the shell of a fresh coconut, although this is often referred to as coconut milk. Canned coconut milk, used in South-east Asian curries, is much thicker and creamier and is made by steeping shredded coconut flesh in water.

1

Mouth-watering Meat & Poultry

beef madras

SERVES 4–6

1–2 dried red chillies

2 tsp ground coriander

2 tsp ground turmeric

1 tsp black mustard seeds

½ tsp ground ginger

¼ tsp ground pepper

140 g/5 oz creamed coconut, grated and dissolved in 300 ml/ 10 fl oz boiling water

55 g/2 oz ghee or 4 tbsp vegetable or groundnut oil

2 onions, chopped

3 large garlic cloves, chopped

700 g/1 lb 9 oz lean stewing steak, such as chuck, trimmed and cut into 5-cm/2-inch cubes

250 ml/9 fl oz beef stock

lemon juice

salt

sprigs of fresh coriander, to garnish

freshly cooked rice, to serve

1 Depending on how hot you want this dish to be, chop the chillies with or without any seeds. The more seeds you include, the hotter the dish will be. Put the chopped chillies and any seeds in a small bowl with the ground coriander, turmeric, mustard seeds, ginger and pepper and stir in a little of the coconut mixture to make a thin paste.

2 Heat the ghee in a large frying pan with a tight-fitting lid over a medium–high heat. Add the onions and garlic and cook for 5–8 minutes, stirring frequently, until the onions are golden brown. Add the spice paste and stir around for 2 minutes, or until the aromas are released.

3 Add the meat and stock and bring to the boil. Reduce the heat to its lowest level, cover tightly and simmer for 1½ hours, or until the beef is tender. Check occasionally that the meat isn't catching on the base of the pan and stir in a little extra water or stock, if necessary.

4 Uncover the pan and stir in the remaining coconut milk with the lemon juice and salt to taste. Bring to the boil, stirring, then reduce the heat again and simmer, still uncovered, until the sauce reduces slightly. Garnish with sprigs of coriander and serve with freshly cooked rice.

beef korma with almonds

SERVES 6

300 ml/10 fl oz vegetable oil

3 onions, finely chopped

1 kg/2 lb 4 oz lean beef, cubed

1½ tsp garam masala

1½ tsp ground coriander

1½ tsp finely chopped fresh ginger

1½ tsp crushed fresh garlic

1 tsp salt

150 ml/5 fl oz natural yogurt

2 whole cloves

3 green cardamom pods

4 black peppercorns

600 ml/1 pint water

chopped blanched almonds, to garnish

sliced fresh green chillies, to garnish

chopped fresh coriander, to garnish

chapatis, to serve

1 Heat the oil in a large, heavy-based frying pan. Add the onions and stir-fry for 8–10 minutes, until golden. Remove half of the onions and set aside.

2 Add the meat to the remaining onions in the frying pan and stir-fry for 5 minutes. Remove the frying pan from the heat.

3 Mix the garam masala, ground coriander, ginger, garlic, salt and yogurt together in a large bowl. Gradually add the meat to the yogurt and spice mixture and mix to coat the meat on all sides. Place the meat mixture in the frying pan, return to the heat, and stir-fry for 5–7 minutes, or until the mixture is nearly brown.

4 Add the cloves, cardamom pods and peppercorns. Add the water, reduce the heat, cover and simmer for 45–60 minutes. If the water has completely evaporated, but the meat is still not tender enough, add another 300 ml/ 10 fl oz water and cook for a further 10–15 minutes, stirring occasionally. Transfer to warmed serving dishes and garnish with the reserved onions, chopped almonds, chillies and fresh coriander. Serve with chapatis.

beef balti

SERVES 4

2 tbsp ghee or vegetable oil

1 onion, thinly sliced

1 garlic clove, finely chopped

3-cm/1¼-inch piece fresh ginger, grated

2 fresh red chillies, deseeded and finely chopped

450 g/1 lb rump steak, cut into thin strips

1 green pepper, deseeded and thinly sliced

1 yellow pepper, deseeded and thinly sliced

1 tsp ground cumin

1 tbsp garam masala

4 tomatoes, chopped

2 tbsp lemon juice

1 tbsp water

salt

chopped fresh coriander, to garnish

naan bread, to serve

1 Heat 1 tablespoon of the ghee in a preheated wok or large, heavy-based frying pan. Add the onion and cook over a low heat, stirring occasionally, for 8–10 minutes, or until golden. Increase the heat to medium, add the garlic, ginger, chillies and steak and cook, stirring occasionally, for 5 minutes, or until the steak is browned all over. Remove with a slotted spoon, set aside and keep warm.

2 Add the remaining ghee to the wok. Add the peppers and cook over a medium heat, stirring occasionally, for 4 minutes, or until softened. Stir in the cumin and garam masala and cook, stirring, for 1 minute.

3 Add the tomatoes, lemon juice and water, season to taste with salt and simmer, stirring constantly, for 3 minutes. Return the steak mixture to the wok and heat through. Transfer to a warmed serving dish, garnish with coriander and serve immediately with naan bread.

thai spicy beef

SERVES 4

450 g/1 lb beef fillet

2 tbsp Thai soy sauce

2 tbsp Thai fish sauce

2 tbsp vegetable or groundnut oil

3–4 coriander roots, chopped

1 tbsp crushed black peppercorns

2 garlic cloves, chopped

1 tbsp palm sugar or soft, light brown sugar

350 g/12 oz potatoes, diced

150 ml/5 fl oz water

bunch of spring onions, chopped

225 g/8 oz baby spinach leaves

freshly cooked rice or noodles, to serve

1 Cut the beef into thick slices and place in a shallow dish. Put the soy sauce, fish sauce, 1 tablespoon of the oil, the coriander roots, peppercorns, garlic and sugar in a food processor and process to a thick paste. Scrape the paste into the dish and toss the beef in the mixture to coat. Cover with clingfilm and set aside to marinate in the fridge for at least 3 hours, preferably overnight.

2 Heat the remaining oil in a wok. Lift the beef out of the marinade, reserving the marinade, and fry for 3–4 minutes on each side, until browned. Add the reserved marinade and the potatoes with the measured water and gradually bring to the boil. Simmer for 6–8 minutes, or until the potatoes are tender.

3 Add the spring onions and spinach. Cook gently until the greens have wilted. Serve immediately with freshly cooked rice or noodles.

beef dhansak

SERVES 6

2 tbsp ghee or vegetable oil

2 onions, chopped

3 garlic cloves, finely chopped

2 tsp ground coriander

2 tsp ground cumin

2 tsp garam masala

1 tsp ground turmeric

450 g/1 lb courgettes, peeled and chopped, or bitter gourd or pumpkin, peeled, deseeded and chopped

1 aubergine, peeled and chopped

4 curry leaves

225 g/8 oz masoor dahl

1 litre/1¾ pints water

1 kg/2 lb 4 oz stewing or braising steak, diced

salt

fresh coriander leaves, to garnish

freshly cooked rice, to serve

1 Heat the ghee in a large, heavy-based saucepan. Add the onions and garlic and cook over a low heat, stirring occasionally, for 8–10 minutes, or until light golden. Stir in the ground coriander, cumin, garam masala and turmeric and cook, stirring constantly, for 2 minutes.

2 Add the courgettes, aubergine, curry leaves, masoor dahl and water. Bring to the boil, then reduce the heat, cover and simmer for 30 minutes, or until the vegetables are tender. Remove the saucepan from the heat and leave to cool slightly. Transfer the mixture to a food processor, in batches if necessary, and process until smooth. Return the mixture to the saucepan and season to taste with salt.

3 Add the steak to the saucepan and bring to the boil. Reduce the heat, cover and simmer for 1¼ hours. Remove the lid and continue to simmer for a further 30 minutes, or until the sauce is thick and the steak is tender. Garnish with coriander leaves and serve with freshly cooked rice.

beef coconut curry

SERVES 4

1 tbsp ground coriander

1 tbsp ground cumin

3 tbsp massaman curry paste

150 ml/5 fl oz water

75 g/2¾ oz creamed coconut

450 g/1 lb beef fillet, cut into strips

400 ml/14 fl oz coconut milk

50 g/1¾ oz unsalted peanuts, finely chopped

2 tbsp Thai fish sauce

1 tsp palm sugar or soft, light brown sugar

4 fresh kaffir lime leaves

sprigs of fresh coriander, to garnish

freshly cooked rice with chopped fresh coriander, to serve

1 Combine the coriander, cumin and curry paste in a bowl. Pour the measured water into a saucepan, add the creamed coconut and heat until it has dissolved. Add the curry paste mixture and simmer for 1 minute.

2 Add the beef and simmer for 6–8 minutes, then add the coconut milk, peanuts, fish sauce and sugar. Simmer gently for 15–20 minutes, until the meat is tender.

3 Add the lime leaves and simmer for 1–2 minutes. Transfer to warmed serving dishes, garnish with sprigs of coriander and serve with freshly cooked rice with chopped coriander stirred through it.

lamb rogan josh

SERVES 4

350 ml/12 fl oz natural yogurt

½ tsp ground asafoetida, dissolved in 2 tbsp water

700 g/1 lb 9 oz boneless leg of lamb, trimmed and cut into 5-cm/2-inch cubes

2 tomatoes, deseeded and chopped

1 onion, chopped

25 g/1 oz ghee or 2 tbsp vegetable or groundnut oil

1½ tbsp garlic and ginger paste

2 tbsp tomato purée

2 bay leaves

1 tbsp ground coriander

¼–1 tsp chilli powder, ideally Kashmiri chilli powder

½ tsp ground turmeric

1 tsp salt

½ tsp garam masala

1 Put the yogurt in a large bowl and stir in the dissolved asafoetida. Add the lamb and use your hands to rub in all the marinade, then set aside for 30 minutes.

2 Meanwhile, put the tomatoes and onion in a blender and process until blended.

3 Heat the ghee in a flameproof casserole or large frying pan with a tight-fitting lid. Add the garlic and ginger paste and stir around until the aromas are released. Stir in the tomato mixture, tomato purée, bay leaves, coriander, chilli powder and turmeric. Reduce the heat to low and simmer, stirring occasionally, for 5–8 minutes.

4 Add the lamb and salt with any leftover marinade and stir around for 2 minutes. Cover, reduce the heat to low and simmer, stirring occasionally, for 30 minutes. The lamb should give off enough moisture to prevent it catching on the base of the pan, but if the sauce looks too dry, stir in a little water.

5 Sprinkle the lamb with the garam masala, re-cover the pan and continue simmering for 15–20 minutes until the lamb is tender. Serve immediately.

lamb red curry

SERVES 4

2 tbsp vegetable oil

1 large onion, sliced

2 garlic cloves, crushed

500 g/1 lb 2 oz lean boneless leg of lamb, cut into 3-cm/1¼-inch cubes

2 tbsp red curry paste

150 ml/5 fl oz coconut milk

1 tbsp soft light brown sugar

1 large red pepper, deseeded and thickly sliced

150 ml/5 fl oz lamb stock or beef stock

1 tbsp Thai fish sauce

2 tbsp lime juice

225 g/8 oz canned water chestnuts, drained

2 tbsp chopped fresh coriander

2 tbsp chopped fresh basil, plus extra leaves to garnish

salt and pepper

1 Heat a wok over a high heat, then add the oil. Add the onion and garlic and stir-fry for 2–3 minutes until softened. Add the lamb and stir-fry quickly until lightly browned.

2 Stir in the curry paste and cook for a few seconds, then add the coconut milk and sugar and bring to the boil. Reduce the heat and leave to simmer for 15 minutes, stirring occasionally.

3 Stir in the red pepper, stock, fish sauce and lime juice, then cover and simmer for a further 15 minutes, or until the lamb is tender.

4 Add the water chestnuts, coriander and chopped basil and season to taste with salt and pepper. Transfer to warmed serving plates, then garnish with basil leaves and serve immediately.

lamb pasanda

SERVES 4–6

600 g/1 lb 5 oz boneless shoulder or leg of lamb

2 tbsp garlic and ginger paste

55 g/2 oz ghee or 4 tbsp vegetable or groundnut oil

3 large onions, chopped

1 fresh green chilli, deseeded and chopped

2 green cardamom pods, lightly crushed

1 cinnamon stick, broken in half

2 tsp ground coriander

1 tsp ground cumin

1 tsp ground turmeric

250 ml/9 fl oz water

150 ml/5 fl oz double cream

4 tbsp ground almonds

1½ tsp salt

1 tsp garam masala

paprika and toasted flaked almonds, to garnish

freshly cooked rice, to serve

1 Cut the meat into thin slices, then place the slices between clingfilm and pound with a rolling pin or meat mallet to make them even thinner. Put the lamb slices in a bowl, add the garlic and ginger paste and use your hands to rub the paste into the lamb. Cover and set aside in a cool place to marinate for 2 hours.

2 Heat the ghee in a large frying pan with a tight-fitting lid over a medium–high heat. Add the onions and chilli and cook, stirring frequently, for 5–8 minutes until the onions are golden brown. Stir in the cardamom pods, cinnamon stick, coriander, cumin and turmeric and continue stirring for 2 minutes, or until the spices are aromatic.

3 Add the meat to the pan and cook, stirring occasionally, for about 5 minutes until it is brown on all sides and the fat begins to separate. Stir in the water and bring to the boil, still stirring. Reduce the heat to its lowest setting, cover the pan tightly and simmer for 40 minutes, or until the meat is tender.

4 When the lamb is tender, stir the cream and ground almonds together in a bowl. Beat in 6 tablespoons of the hot cooking liquid from the pan, then gradually beat this mixture back into the pan. Stir in the salt and garam masala. Continue to simmer for a further 5 minutes, uncovered, stirring occasionally. Garnish with a sprinkling of paprika and toasted flaked almonds and serve with freshly cooked rice.

lamb do piaza

SERVES 4

4 onions, sliced into rings

3 garlic cloves, roughly chopped

2.5-cm/1-inch piece fresh ginger, grated

1 tsp ground coriander

1 tsp ground cumin

1 tsp chilli powder

½ tsp ground turmeric

1 tsp ground cinnamon

1 tsp garam masala

4 tbsp water

5 tbsp ghee or vegetable oil

600 g/1 lb 5 oz boneless lamb, cut into bite-sized chunks

6 tbsp natural yogurt

salt and pepper

fresh coriander leaves, to garnish

freshly cooked rice, to serve

1 Put half of the onions into a food processor with the garlic, ginger, ground coriander, cumin, chilli powder, turmeric, cinnamon and garam masala. Add the water and process to a paste.

2 Heat 4 tablespoons of the ghee in a saucepan over a medium heat. Add the remaining onions and cook, stirring, for 3 minutes. Remove from the heat. Lift out the onions with a slotted spoon and set aside. Heat the remaining ghee in the pan over a high heat, add the lamb and cook, stirring, for 5 minutes. Lift out the meat and drain on kitchen paper.

3 Add the onion paste to the pan and cook over a medium heat, stirring, until the oil separates. Stir in the yogurt, season to taste with salt and pepper, return the lamb to the pan and stir well.

4 Bring the mixture gently to the boil, reduce the heat, cover and simmer for 25 minutes. Stir in the reserved onion rings and cook for a further 5 minutes. Remove from the heat, and garnish with coriander leaves. Serve immediately with freshly cooked rice.

lamb & spinach curry

SERVES 4

150 ml/5 fl oz vegetable oil

2 onions, sliced

¼ bunch of fresh coriander

2 fresh green chillies, chopped

1½ tsp finely chopped fresh ginger

1½ tsp crushed fresh garlic

1 tsp chilli powder

½ tsp ground turmeric

450 g/1 lb lean lamb, cut into bite-sized chunks

½ tsp salt

1 kg/2 lb 4 oz fresh spinach, trimmed, washed and chopped

350 ml/12 fl oz water

finely chopped fresh red chilli, to garnish

1 Heat the oil in a large, heavy-based saucepan. Add the onions and cook until light golden.

2 Add the fresh coriander and green chillies to the saucepan and stir-fry for 3–5 minutes. Reduce the heat and add the ginger, garlic, chilli powder and turmeric, stirring well.

3 Add the lamb to the saucepan and stir-fry for a further 5 minutes. Add the salt and the spinach and cook, stirring occasionally with a wooden spoon, for a further 3–5 minutes.

4 Add the water, stirring, and cook over a low heat, covered, for 45 minutes. Remove the lid and check the meat. If it is not tender, turn the meat over, increase the heat and cook, uncovered, until the surplus water has been absorbed.

5 Transfer the lamb and spinach mixture to a warmed serving dish and garnish with chopped red chilli. Serve hot.

kashmiri kofta curry

SERVES 4

500g/1 lb 2 oz lean minced lamb

1 garlic clove, crushed

2.5-cm/1-inch piece fresh ginger, grated

1 fresh red chilli, deseeded and very finely chopped

4 tbsp chopped fresh coriander

2 tbsp vegetable oil

1 large onion, finely chopped

2 tbsp garam masala

300 ml/10 fl oz water

4 tbsp mango chutney

150 ml/5 fl oz natural yogurt

salt and pepper

naan bread or chapatis, to serve

1 Mix together the minced lamb, garlic, ginger, chilli, 2 tablespoons of fresh coriander and season to taste in a bowl until well combined. Form into 20 small balls and set aside.

2 Heat the vegetable oil over a medium heat in a non-stick frying pan. Add the meatballs and fry for 10 minutes, turning to brown on all sides. Add the onion and cook for 3 minutes until the onion is starting to soften. Add the garam masala and fry for a further minute.

3 Add the water and mango chutney and allow to simmer for 10 minutes. Stir in the yogurt and heat through but do not allow to boil as the mixture could curdle.

4 Serve sprinkled with the remaining coriander, accompanied by naan bread or chapatis.

lamb, tomato & aubergine curry

SERVES 4

2 tbsp vegetable oil

500 g/1 lb 2 oz lamb fillet
or leg, cut into cubes

1 large onion, roughly
chopped

2–3 tbsp curry paste

1 aubergine, cut into small
cubes

10 tomatoes, peeled,
deseeded and roughly
chopped

400 ml/14 fl oz coconut
milk

300 ml/10 fl oz lamb stock

2 tbsp chopped fresh
coriander, plus extra
sprigs to garnish

naan bread, to serve

1 Heat the oil in a large frying pan. Add the lamb in batches and cook for 8–10 minutes, or until browned all over. Remove with a slotted spoon and set aside.

2 Add the onion to the frying pan and cook for 2–3 minutes, or until just softened. Add the curry paste and stir-fry for a further 2 minutes. Add the aubergine, three-quarters of the tomatoes and the lamb and stir together.

3 Add the coconut milk and stock and simmer gently for 30–40 minutes, until the lamb is tender and the curry has thickened.

4 Mix the remaining tomatoes and the chopped coriander together in a small bowl, then stir into the curry. Garnish with sprigs of coriander and serve immediately with naan bread.

pork vindaloo

SERVES 4–6

4 tbsp mustard oil

2 large onions, finely chopped

6 bay leaves

6 cloves

6 garlic cloves, chopped

3 green cardamom pods, lightly cracked

1–2 small fresh red chillies, chopped

2 tbsp ground cumin

½ tsp salt

½ tsp ground turmeric

2 tbsp cider vinegar

2 tbsp water

1 tbsp tomato purée

700 g/1 lb 9 oz boneless shoulder of pork, trimmed and cut into 5-cm/2-inch cubes

1 Put the mustard oil in a large frying pan or saucepan with a tight-fitting lid over a high heat until it smokes. Turn off the heat and leave the mustard oil to cool completely.

2 Reheat the oil over a medium–high heat. Add the onions and cook, stirring frequently, for 5–8 minutes until softened but not coloured.

3 Add the bay leaves, cloves, garlic, cardamom pods, chillies, cumin, salt, turmeric and 1 tablespoon of the vinegar to the onions and stir around. Stir in the water, then cover the pan and simmer for about 1 minute, or until the water is absorbed and the fat separates.

4 Dissolve the tomato purée in the remaining vinegar, then stir it into the pan. Add the pork and stir around. Add just enough water to cover the pork and bring to the boil. Reduce the heat to its lowest level, cover the pan tightly and simmer for 40–60 minutes until the pork is tender.

5 If too much liquid remains in the pan when the pork is tender, use a slotted spoon to remove the pork from the pan and boil the liquid until it reduces to the required amount. Return the pork to the pan to heat through, then transfer to warmed dishes and serve.

pork with spices

SERVES 4

1 tsp ground coriander

1 tsp ground cumin

1 tsp chilli powder

1 tbsp dried fenugreek
leaves (methi)

1 tsp ground fenugreek

150 ml/5 fl oz natural
yogurt

450 g/1 lb diced pork fillet

4 tbsp ghee or vegetable oil

1 large onion, sliced

5-cm/2-inch piece fresh
ginger, finely chopped

4 garlic cloves, finely
chopped

1 cinnamon stick

6 cardamom pods

6 whole cloves

2 bay leaves

175 ml/6 fl oz water

salt

1 Mix the coriander, cumin, chilli powder, dried fenugreek, ground fenugreek and yogurt together in a small bowl. Place the pork in a large, shallow, non-metallic dish and add the spice mixture, turning well to coat. Cover with clingfilm and leave to marinate in the refrigerator for 30 minutes.

2 Heat the ghee in a large, heavy-based saucepan. Cook the onion over a low heat, stirring occasionally, for 5 minutes, or until softened. Add the ginger, garlic, cinnamon stick, cardamom pods, cloves and bay leaves and cook, stirring constantly, for 2 minutes, or until the spices give off their aroma. Add the meat with its marinade and the water, and season to taste with salt. Bring to the boil, reduce the heat, cover and simmer for 30 minutes.

3 Transfer the meat mixture to a preheated wok or large, heavy-based frying pan and cook over a low heat, stirring constantly, until dry and tender. If necessary, occasionally sprinkle with a little water to prevent it sticking to the wok. Serve immediately.

pork with tamarind

SERVES 6

55 g/2 oz dried tamarind, chopped

500 ml/18 fl oz boiling water

2 fresh green chillies, deseeded and roughly chopped

2 onions, roughly chopped

2 garlic cloves, roughly chopped

1 lemon grass stalk, bulb end roughly chopped

2 tbsp ghee or vegetable oil

1 tbsp ground coriander

1 tsp ground turmeric

1 tsp ground cardamom

1 tsp chilli powder

1 tsp ginger paste

1 cinnamon stick

1 kg/2 lb 4 oz diced pork fillet

1 tbsp chopped fresh coriander

sprigs of fresh coriander, to garnish

sliced fresh red chillies, to garnish

naan bread, to serve

1 Place the dried tamarind in a small bowl, pour in the boiling water and mix well. Leave to soak for 30 minutes.

2 Sieve the soaking liquid into a clean bowl, pressing down the tamarind pulp with the back of a wooden spoon. Discard the pulp. Pour 1 tablespoon of the tamarind liquid into a food processor and add the green chillies, onions, garlic and lemon grass and process until smooth.

3 Heat the ghee in a large, heavy-based saucepan. Add the ground coriander, turmeric, cardamom, chilli powder, ginger paste, cinnamon stick and the chilli and onion paste, then cook, stirring, for 2 minutes, or until the spices give off their aroma.

4 Add the pork and cook, stirring constantly, until lightly browned and well coated in the spice mixture. Pour in the remaining tamarind liquid, bring to the boil, then reduce the heat, cover and simmer for 30 minutes. Remove the lid from the saucepan and simmer for a further 30 minutes, or until the pork is tender. Stir in the chopped coriander. Garnish with sprigs of coriander and sliced red chillies and serve with naan bread.

pork red curry with peppers

SERVES 4

2 tbsp vegetable or groundnut oil

1 onion, roughly chopped

2 garlic cloves, chopped

450 g/1 lb pork fillet, thickly sliced

1 red pepper, deseeded and cut into squares

175 g/6 oz mushrooms, quartered

2 tbsp red curry paste

115 g/4 oz creamed coconut, chopped

300 ml/10 fl oz pork or vegetable stock

2 tbsp Thai soy sauce

4 tomatoes, peeled, deseeded and chopped

handful of chopped fresh coriander

1 Heat the oil in a wok or large frying pan and cook the onion and garlic for 1–2 minutes, until they are softened but not browned.

2 Add the pork slices and stir-fry for 2–3 minutes until browned all over. Add the pepper, mushrooms and curry paste.

3 Dissolve the coconut in the stock and add to the wok with the soy sauce. Bring to the boil and simmer for 4–5 minutes until the liquid has reduced and thickened.

4 Add the tomatoes and coriander and cook for 1–2 minutes before serving.

chicken jalfrezi

SERVES 4

½ tsp cumin seeds

½ tsp coriander seeds

1 tsp mustard oil

3 tbsp vegetable oil

1 large onion, finely chopped

3 garlic cloves, crushed

1 tbsp tomato purée

2 tomatoes, peeled and chopped

1 tsp ground turmeric

½ tsp chilli powder

½ tsp garam masala

1 tsp red wine vinegar

1 small red pepper, deseeded and chopped

125 g/4½ oz frozen broad beans

500 g/1 lb 2 oz cooked chicken, chopped

salt

sprigs of fresh coriander, to garnish

freshly cooked rice, to serve

1 Grind the cumin and coriander seeds in a mortar with a pestle, then set aside. Heat the mustard oil in a large, heavy-based frying pan over a high heat for 1 minute, or until it begins to smoke. Add the vegetable oil, reduce the heat and add the onion and garlic. Cook for 10 minutes, or until golden.

2 Add the tomato purée, tomatoes, turmeric, chilli powder, garam masala, vinegar and reserved ground cumin and coriander seeds to the frying pan. Stir the mixture until fragrant.

3 Add the red pepper and broad beans and stir for a further 2 minutes, or until the pepper is softened. Stir in the chicken, and season to taste with salt. Simmer gently for 6–8 minutes, or until the chicken is heated through and the beans are tender. Transfer to warmed serving bowls, garnish with sprigs of coriander and serve with freshly cooked rice.

chicken balti

SERVES 6

3 tbsp ghee or vegetable oil

2 large onions, sliced

3 tomatoes, sliced

½ tsp kalonji seeds

4 black peppercorns

2 cardamom pods

1 cinnamon stick

1 tsp chilli powder

1 tsp garam masala

2 tsp garlic and ginger paste

700 g/1 lb 9 oz skinless, boneless chicken breasts or thighs, diced

2 tbsp natural yogurt

2 tbsp chopped fresh coriander, plus extra sprigs to garnish

2 fresh green chillies, deseeded and finely chopped

2 tbsp lime juice

salt

1 Heat the ghee in a large, heavy-based frying pan. Add the onions and cook over a low heat, stirring occasionally, for 10 minutes, or until golden. Add the tomatoes, kalonji seeds, peppercorns, cardamom pods, cinnamon stick, chilli powder, garam masala, and garlic and ginger paste, and season to taste with salt. Cook, stirring constantly, for 5 minutes.

2 Add the chicken and cook, stirring constantly, for 5 minutes, or until well coated in the spice paste. Stir in the yogurt. Cover and simmer, stirring occasionally, for 10 minutes.

3 Stir in the chopped coriander, chillies and lime juice. Transfer to a warmed serving dish, garnish with sprigs of coriander and serve immediately.

chicken with mushrooms & beans

SERVES 4–6

2 tsp garam masala

1 tsp mild, medium or hot curry powder, to taste

1 tbsp water

55 g/2 oz ghee or 4 tbsp vegetable or groundnut oil

8 skinless, boneless chicken thighs, sliced

1 small onion, chopped

2 large garlic cloves, crushed

100 g/3½ oz green beans, topped and tailed and chopped

100 g/3½ oz mushrooms, thickly sliced

2 tbsp milk

salt and pepper

sprigs of fresh coriander, to garnish

freshly cooked rice, to serve

1 To make the curry paste, put the garam masala and curry powder in a bowl and stir in the water, then set aside.

2 Melt half the ghee in a large, heavy-based saucepan or frying pan with a tight-fitting lid over a medium–high heat. Add the chicken pieces and curry paste and stir for 5 minutes.

3 Add the onion, garlic and green beans and continue cooking for a further 5 minutes until the chicken is cooked through.

4 Add the remaining ghee and mushrooms and, when the ghee melts, stir in the milk. Season to taste with salt and pepper. Reduce the heat to low, cover and simmer for 10 minutes, stirring occasionally. Garnish with sprigs of coriander and serve immediately with freshly cooked rice.

chicken korma

SERVES 4

**1 chicken, weighing
1.3 kg/3 lb**

225 g/8 oz ghee or butter

3 onions, thinly sliced

1 garlic clove, crushed

**2.5-cm/1-inch piece fresh
ginger, grated**

1 tsp mild chilli powder

1 tsp ground turmeric

1 tsp ground coriander

½ tsp ground cardamom

½ tsp ground cinnamon

½ tsp salt

1 tbsp gram flour

125 ml/4 fl oz milk

**500 ml/18 fl oz double
cream**

**fresh coriander leaves,
to garnish**

**freshly cooked rice,
to serve**

1 Put the chicken into a large saucepan, cover with water and bring to the boil. Reduce the heat, cover and simmer for 30 minutes. Remove from the heat, lift out the chicken and set aside to cool. Set aside 125 ml/4 fl oz of the cooking liquid. Remove and discard the skin and bones. Cut the flesh into bite-sized pieces.

2 Heat the ghee in a large saucepan over a medium heat. Add the onions and garlic and cook, stirring, for 3 minutes, or until softened. Add the ginger, chilli powder, turmeric, ground coriander, cardamom, cinnamon and salt and cook for a further 5 minutes. Add the chicken and the reserved cooking liquid. Cook for 2 minutes.

3 Blend the flour with a little of the milk and add to the pan, then stir in the remaining milk. Bring to the boil, stirring, then reduce the heat, cover and simmer for 25 minutes. Stir in the cream, cover and simmer for a further 15 minutes.

4 Garnish with coriander leaves and serve with freshly cooked rice.

chicken tikka masala

SERVES 4–6

**30 g/1 oz ghee or 2 tbsp
vegetable or groundnut
oil**

**1 large garlic clove, finely
chopped**

**1 fresh red chilli, deseeded
and chopped**

2 tsp ground cumin

2 tsp paprika

**400 g/14 oz canned
chopped tomatoes**

**300 ml/10 fl oz double
cream**

**8 pieces cooked tandoori
chicken**

salt and pepper

**sprigs of fresh coriander,
to garnish**

1 To make the tikka masala, heat the ghee in a large frying pan with a lid over a medium heat. Add the garlic and chilli and stir-fry for 1 minute. Stir in the cumin, paprika, and salt and pepper to taste and continue stirring for about 30 seconds.

2 Stir the tomatoes with their juices and the cream into the pan. Reduce the heat to low and leave the sauce to simmer for about 10 minutes, stirring frequently, until it reduces and thickens.

3 Meanwhile, remove all the bones and any skin from the tandoori chicken pieces, then cut the meat into bite-sized pieces.

4 Adjust the seasoning of the sauce, if necessary. Add the chicken pieces to the pan, cover and leave to simmer for 3–5 minutes until the chicken is heated through. Garnish with sprigs of coriander to serve.

chicken thai red curry

SERVES 2–4

6 garlic cloves, chopped

2 fresh red chillies, chopped

2 tbsp chopped lemon grass

1 tsp finely grated lime rind

1 tbsp chopped fresh kaffir lime leaves

1 tbsp red curry paste

1 tbsp coriander seeds

1 tbsp chilli oil

4 skinless, boneless chicken breasts, sliced

300 ml/10 fl oz coconut milk

300 ml/10 fl oz chicken stock

1 tbsp soy sauce

55 g/2 oz ground peanuts

3 spring onions, sliced

1 red pepper, deseeded and sliced

1 large aubergine, sliced

chopped fresh coriander, to garnish

freshly cooked rice, to serve

1 Place the garlic, chillies, lemon grass, lime rind, lime leaves, curry paste and coriander seeds in a food processor and process until the mixture is smooth.

2 Heat the oil in a preheated wok or large frying pan over a high heat. Add the chicken and the garlic mixture and stir-fry for 5 minutes. Add the coconut milk, stock and soy sauce and bring to the boil. Reduce the heat and cook, stirring, for a further 3 minutes. Stir in the ground peanuts and simmer for 20 minutes.

3 Add the spring onions, red pepper and aubergine and leave to simmer, stirring occasionally, for a further 10 minutes. Garnish with coriander and serve with freshly cooked rice.

chicken thai green curry

SERVES 4

2 tbsp groundnut or sunflower oil

2 tbsp green curry paste

500 g/1 lb 2 oz skinless, boneless chicken breasts, cut into cubes

2 fresh kaffir lime leaves, roughly torn

1 lemon grass stalk, finely chopped

225 ml/8 fl oz coconut milk

16 baby aubergines, halved

2 tbsp Thai fish sauce

sprigs of fresh Thai basil and thinly sliced kaffir lime leaves, to garnish

1 Heat the oil in a preheated wok or large, heavy-based frying pan. Add the curry paste and stir-fry briefly until all the aromas are released.

2 Add the chicken, lime leaves and lemon grass and stir-fry for 3–4 minutes, until the meat is beginning to colour. Add the coconut milk and aubergines and simmer gently for 8–10 minutes, or until tender.

3 Stir in the fish sauce and serve immediately, garnished with sprigs of Thai basil and lime leaves.

VARIATION

Replace the baby aubergines with 3 green peppers, sliced, which will enhance the green colour of the curry.

Flavoursome Fish & Seafood

fish korma

SERVES 4

**700 g/1 lb 9 oz tilapia
fillets, cut into 5-cm/
2-inch pieces**

1 tbsp lemon juice

1 tsp salt

**55 g/2 oz raw unsalted
cashew nuts**

3 tbsp sunflower or olive oil

**5-cm/2-inch piece
cinnamon stick, halved**

**4 green cardamom pods,
bruised**

2 cloves

**1 large onion, finely
chopped**

**1–2 fresh green chillies,
chopped**

2 tsp ginger paste

2 tsp garlic paste

150 ml/5 fl oz single cream

55 g/2 oz natural yogurt

¼ tsp ground turmeric

½ tsp sugar

**1 tbsp toasted flaked
almonds, to garnish**

naan bread, to serve

1 Place the fish on a large plate and gently rub in the
lemon juice and ½ teaspoon of the salt. Set aside for
20 minutes. Put the cashews in a bowl, cover with boiling
water and leave to soak for 15 minutes.

2 Heat the oil in a wide shallow pan over a low heat and
add the cinnamon, cardamom and cloves. Let them sizzle
for 30–40 seconds.

3 Add the onion, chillies and ginger and garlic pastes.
Increase the heat slightly and cook, stirring frequently,
for 9–10 minutes, until the onion is very soft.

4 Meanwhile, drain the cashews. Put them in a food
processor with the cream and yogurt and process to a
thick purée.

5 Stir the turmeric into the onion mixture and add the
puréed ingredients, the remaining salt and the sugar.
Mix thoroughly and arrange the fish in the sauce in a single
layer. Bring to a slow simmer, cover the pan and cook for
5 minutes. Remove the lid and shake the pan gently from
side to side. Spoon some of the sauce over the pieces of fish.
Re-cover and cook for a further 3–4 minutes.

6 Transfer to a warmed serving dish and garnish with the
toasted almonds. Serve with naan bread.

cod curry

SERVES 4

1 tbsp vegetable oil

1 small onion, chopped

2 garlic cloves, chopped

2.5-cm/1-inch piece fresh ginger, roughly chopped

2 large ripe tomatoes, peeled and roughly chopped

150 ml/5 fl oz fish stock

1 tbsp medium curry paste

1 tsp ground coriander

400 g/14 oz canned chickpeas, drained and rinsed

750 g/1 lb 10 oz cod fillet, cut into large chunks

4 tbsp chopped fresh coriander

4 tbsp thick natural yogurt

salt and pepper

freshly cooked rice, to serve

1 Heat the oil in a large saucepan over a low heat. Add the onion, garlic and ginger and cook for 4–5 minutes until softened. Remove from the heat. Put the onion mixture into a food processor or blender with the tomatoes and fish stock and process until smooth.

2 Return to the saucepan with the curry paste, ground coriander and chickpeas. Mix together well, then simmer gently for 15 minutes until thickened.

3 Add the pieces of fish and return to a simmer. Cook for 5 minutes until the fish is just tender. Remove from the heat and leave to stand for 2–3 minutes.

4 Stir in the coriander and yogurt. Season to taste with salt and pepper and serve with freshly cooked rice.

fish curry with rice noodles

SERVES 4

2 tbsp vegetable or groundnut oil

1 large onion, chopped

2 garlic cloves, chopped

85 g/3 oz button mushrooms

225 g/8 oz monkfish, cut into 2.5-cm/1-inch cubes

225 g/8 oz salmon fillets, cut into 2.5-cm/1-inch cubes

225 g/8 oz cod, cut into 2.5-cm/1-inch cubes

2 tbsp red curry paste

400 g/14 oz coconut milk

handful of chopped fresh coriander

1 tsp palm sugar or soft, light brown sugar

1 tsp Thai fish sauce

115 g/4 oz rice noodles

3 spring onions, chopped

55 g/2 oz beansprouts

a few fresh Thai basil leaves

1 Heat the oil in a wok or large frying pan and gently fry the onion, garlic and mushrooms until softened but not browned.

2 Add the fish, curry paste and coconut milk and bring gently to the boil. Simmer for 2–3 minutes before adding the coriander, sugar and fish sauce. Keep warm.

3 Meanwhile, soak the noodles for 3–4 minutes (or according to the packet instructions) or until tender and drain well through a colander. Put the colander and noodles over a saucepan of simmering water. Add the spring onions, beansprouts and basil and steam on top of the noodles for 1–2 minutes or until just wilted.

4 Pile the noodles into warmed serving dishes, top with the fish curry and serve immediately.

thai steamed seabass curry

SERVES 4

100 g/3½ oz creamed coconut

150 ml/5 fl oz boiling water

2 tbsp green curry paste

1 tbsp Thai fish sauce

1 egg, beaten

450 g/1 lb seabass fillets, skinned and cut into 5-cm/2-inch pieces

1 tbsp roughly chopped fresh coriander

1 tbsp roughly chopped fresh mint

1 tbsp roughly chopped fresh basil

4 fresh kaffir lime leaves, finely shredded

freshly cooked Thai fragrant rice, to serve

1 Place the creamed coconut in a bowl, add the boiling water and mix to a paste. Add the curry paste, fish sauce and egg and beat to combine with a fork.

2 Place the seabass pieces together with the chopped herbs and kaffir lime leaves in a heat-proof non-metallic bowl.

3 Pour the coconut mixture over the fish pieces, cover the bowl with foil and place it in a steamer over a pan of boiling water. Steam for 15 minutes, stir carefully, recover and cook for a further 5 minutes until the fish is just cooked through and the sauce is lightly set.

4 Serve hot with freshly cooked Thai fragrant rice.

fish balti

SERVES 4–6

½ tbsp garlic and ginger
paste

1 fresh green chilli,
deseeded and chopped

1 tsp ground coriander

1 tsp ground cumin

½ tsp ground turmeric

½ tsp chilli powder

1 tbsp water

900 g/2 lb thick fish fillets,
such as monkfish, grey
mullet, cod or haddock,
rinsed and cut into large
chunks

2 bay leaves, torn

140 g/5 oz ghee or
150 ml/5 fl oz vegetable
or groundnut oil

2 large onions, chopped

150 ml/5 fl oz water

salt

sprigs of fresh coriander,
to garnish

1 To make the marinade, mix the garlic and ginger paste,
green chilli, ground coriander, cumin, turmeric and chilli
powder together with salt to taste in a large bowl. Gradually
stir in the water to form a thin paste. Add the fish chunks and
smear with the marinade. Tuck the bay leaves underneath and
leave to marinate in the refrigerator for at least 30 minutes,
or up to 4 hours.

2 When you are ready to cook the fish, remove from the
refrigerator 15 minutes in advance. Heat the ghee in a
wok or large frying pan over a medium–high heat. Add the
onions, sprinkle with a ½ tablespoon of salt and cook, stirring
frequently, for 8 minutes, or until very soft and golden.

3 Gently add the fish, bay leaves, and marinade to the pan
and stir in the water. Bring to the boil, then immediately
reduce the heat and cook the fish for 4–5 minutes, spooning
the sauce over the fish and carefully moving the chunks
around, until they are cooked through and flake easily.
Transfer to warmed dishes and serve garnished with sprigs
of coriander.

bengali-style fish

1 tsp ground turmeric

1 tsp salt

1 kg/2 lb 4 oz cod fillet, skinned and cut into pieces

6 tbsp mustard oil

4 fresh green chillies

1 tsp finely chopped fresh ginger

1 tsp crushed fresh garlic

2 onions, finely chopped

2 tomatoes, finely chopped

450 ml/16 fl oz water

chopped fresh coriander, to garnish

naan bread, to serve

1 Mix the turmeric and salt together in a small bowl, then spoon the mixture over the fish pieces.

2 Heat the mustard oil in a large, heavy-based frying pan. Add the fish and fry until pale yellow. Remove the fish with a slotted spoon and set aside.

3 Place the chillies, ginger, garlic, onions and tomatoes in a mortar and grind with a pestle to make a paste. Alternatively, place the ingredients in a food processor and process until smooth.

4 Transfer the spice paste to a clean frying pan and dry-fry until golden brown.

5 Remove the frying pan from the heat and place the fish pieces in the paste without breaking up the fish. Return the frying pan to the heat, add the water and cook over a medium heat for 15–20 minutes. Transfer to a warmed serving dish, garnish with chopped coriander and serve with naan bread.

fish thai green curry

SERVES 4

2 tbsp vegetable oil

1 garlic clove, chopped

2 tbsp green curry paste

1 small aubergine, diced

125 ml/4 fl oz coconut milk

2 tbsp Thai fish sauce

1 tsp sugar

225 g/8 oz firm white fish fillets, cut into pieces

125 ml/4 fl oz fish stock

2 fresh kaffir lime leaves, finely shredded

about 15 fresh Thai basil leaves

sprigs of fresh dill, to garnish

1 Heat the vegetable oil in a large frying pan or preheated wok over a medium heat until almost smoking. Add the garlic and cook until golden. Add the curry paste and stir-fry a few seconds before adding the aubergine. Stir-fry for about 4–5 minutes until softened.

2 Add the coconut milk, bring to the boil and stir until it thickens and curdles slightly. Add the fish sauce and sugar to the frying pan and stir well.

3 Add the fish pieces and stock. Simmer for 3–4 minutes, stirring occasionally, until the fish is just tender. Add the lime leaves and basil, then cook for a further 1 minute. Transfer to a warmed serving dish and garnish with a few sprigs of fresh dill. Serve immediately.

thai monkfish & salmon

SERVES 4

juice of 1 lime

4 tbsp Thai fish sauce

2 tbsp Thai soy sauce

1 fresh red chilli, deseeded and chopped

350 g/12 oz monkfish fillet, cut into cubes

350 g/12 oz salmon fillets, skinned and cut into cubes

400 ml/14 fl oz coconut milk

3 fresh kaffir lime leaves

1 tbsp red curry paste

1 lemon grass stalk (white part only), finely chopped

freshly cooked jasmine rice with chopped fresh coriander, to serve

1 Combine the lime juice, half the fish sauce and all of the soy sauce in a shallow non-metallic dish. Add the chilli and the fish, stir to coat, cover with clingfilm and chill for 1–2 hours, or overnight.

2 Bring the coconut milk to the boil in a saucepan and add the lime leaves, curry paste, the remaining fish sauce and the lemon grass. Simmer gently for 10–15 minutes.

3 Add the fish with its marinade and simmer gently for 4–5 minutes, until the fish is cooked. Serve hot accompanied by freshly cooked jasmine rice with chopped coriander stirred through it.

mixed seafood in coconut milk

SERVES 4

2 tbsp vegetable or groundnut oil

6 spring onions, roughly chopped

2.5-cm/1-inch piece fresh ginger, grated

2–3 tbsp red curry paste

400 ml/14 fl oz coconut milk

150 ml/5 fl oz fish stock

4 fresh kaffir lime leaves

1 lemon grass stalk, broken in half

350 g/12 oz white fish fillets, skinned and cut into chunks

225 g/8 oz squid rings and tentacles, cleaned

225 g/8 oz large cooked peeled prawns

1 tbsp Thai fish sauce

2 tbsp Thai soy sauce

4 tbsp snipped fresh Chinese chives

freshly cooked rice, to serve

1 Heat the oil in a wok or large frying pan and stir-fry the spring onions and ginger for 1–2 minutes. Add the curry paste and stir-fry for 1–2 minutes.

2 Add the coconut milk, fish stock, lime leaves and lemon grass. Bring to the boil, then lower the heat and simmer for 1 minute.

3 Add the fish, squid and prawns and simmer for 2–3 minutes, until the fish is cooked. Add the fish sauce and soy sauce and stir in the chives. Serve immediately with freshly cooked rice.

mixed seafood curry

SERVES 4

1 tbsp vegetable or
groundnut oil

3 shallots, finely chopped

2.5-cm/1-inch piece fresh
galangal, peeled and
thinly sliced

2 garlic cloves, finely
chopped

400 ml/14 fl oz coconut
milk

2 lemon grass stalks,
snapped in half

4 tbsp Thai fish sauce

2 tbsp chilli sauce

225 g/8 oz raw tiger
prawns, peeled and
deveined

225 g/8 oz baby squid,
cleaned and thickly
sliced

225 g/8 oz salmon fillet,
skinned and cut into
chunks

175 g/6 oz tuna steak,
cut into chunks

225 g/8 oz fresh mussels,
scrubbed and debearded

fresh Chinese chives,
to garnish

freshly cooked rice,
to serve

1 Heat the oil in a large wok with a tight-fitting lid and stir-fry the shallots, galangal and garlic for 1–2 minutes, until they start to soften. Add the coconut milk, lemon grass, fish sauce and chilli sauce. Bring to the boil, lower the heat and simmer for 1–2 minutes.

2 Add the prawns, squid, salmon and tuna and simmer for 3–4 minutes, until the prawns have turned pink and the fish is cooked.

3 Discard any mussels with broken shells or any that refuse to close when tapped with a knife. Add the remaining mussels to the wok and cover with a lid. Simmer for 1–2 minutes, until they have opened. Discard any mussels that remain closed. Garnish with Chinese chives and serve immediately with freshly cooked rice.

goan-style seafood curry

SERVES 4-6

3 tbsp vegetable or groundnut oil

1 tbsp black mustard seeds

12 fresh curry leaves or 1 tbsp dried curry leaves

6 shallots, finely chopped

1 garlic clove, crushed

1 tsp ground turmeric

½ tsp ground coriander

¼–½ tsp chilli powder

140 g/5 oz creamed coconut, grated and dissolved in 300 ml/ 10 fl oz boiling water

500 g/1 lb 2 oz skinless, boneless white fish, such as monkfish or cod, cut into large chunks

450 g/1 lb large raw prawns, peeled and deveined

finely grated rind and juice of 1 lime

salt

lime slices, to serve

1 Heat the oil in a wok or large frying pan over a high heat. Add the mustard seeds and stir them around for about 1 minute, or until they pop. Stir in the curry leaves.

2 Add the shallots and garlic and stir for about 5 minutes, or until the shallots are golden. Stir in the turmeric, coriander and chilli powder and continue stirring for about 30 seconds.

3 Add the dissolved creamed coconut. Bring to the boil, then reduce the heat to medium and stir for about 2 minutes.

4 Reduce the heat to low, add the fish and simmer for 1 minute, spooning the sauce over the fish and very gently stirring it around. Add the prawns and continue to simmer for 4–5 minutes longer until the fish flakes easily and the prawns turn pink and curl.

5 Add half the lime juice, then taste and add more lime juice and salt to taste. Sprinkle with the lime rind and serve with lime slices.

seafood & mango curry

SERVES 4

2 tbsp groundnut oil

1 red onion, finely chopped

2 garlic cloves, crushed

4 tbsp mild curry paste

400 ml/14 fl oz coconut milk

grated rind of 1 lime

3 tbsp ground almonds

400 g/14 oz frozen mixed seafood, defrosted and drained

1 small ripe mango, peeled, stoned and diced

2 tbsp roughly chopped fresh coriander, to garnish

1 Heat the groundnut oil in a heavy-based pan over a medium heat. Add the onion and garlic and fry for 4 minutes to soften. Add the curry paste and cook for a further 2 minutes, stirring occasionally.

2 Add the coconut milk and grated lime rind and simmer for 3 minutes. Add the ground almonds and defrosted seafood. Return the pan to the boil then reduce the heat and allow to simmer for 3 minutes until seafood is just cooked through.

3 Stir in the diced mango and continue to simmer for 1 minute to heat through. Garnish with chopped coriander and serve hot.

mixed seafood noodles

SERVES 4

2 tbsp groundnut or vegetable oil

6 spring onions, cut into 2.5-cm/1-inch lengths

1 large carrot, cut into matchsticks

55 g/2 oz green beans, trimmed and cut into short lengths

2 tbsp red curry paste

700 ml/1¼ pints coconut milk

225 g/8 oz skinned white fish fillet, such as cod or coley, cut into 2.5-cm/ 1-inch cubes

225 g/8 oz squid, cleaned and cut into thick rings

225 g/8 oz large raw prawns, peeled and deveined

55 g/2 oz fresh beansprouts

115 g/4 oz dried rice noodles, cooked and drained

handful of fresh coriander, chopped

handful of fresh Thai basil leaves, to garnish

1 Heat the oil in a preheated wok, add the spring onions, carrot and green beans and stir-fry over a medium–high heat for 2–3 minutes until starting to soften.

2 Stir in the curry paste, then add the coconut milk. Bring gently to the boil, stirring occasionally, then reduce the heat and simmer for 2–3 minutes. Add all the fish, squid, prawns and beansprouts and simmer for 2–3 minutes until just cooked through and the prawns have turned pink.

3 Stir in the cooked noodles and coriander and cook for 1 minute. Serve immediately, scattered with the basil.

tandoori prawns

SERVES 4

4 tbsp natural yogurt

2 fresh green chillies, deseeded and chopped

½ tbsp garlic and ginger paste

seeds from 4 green cardamom pods

2 tsp ground cumin

1 tsp tomato purée

¼ tsp ground turmeric

¼ tsp salt

pinch of chilli powder, ideally Kashmiri chilli powder

24 raw tiger prawns, thawed if frozen, peeled, deveined and tails left intact

oil, for greasing

1 Put the yogurt, green chillies and garlic and ginger paste in a small food processor or spice grinder and process to a smooth paste. Transfer the paste to a large non-metallic bowl and stir in the cardamom seeds, cumin, tomato purée, turmeric, salt and chilli powder.

2 Add the prawns to the bowl and use your hands to make sure they are coated with the yogurt marinade. Cover the bowl with clingfilm and chill for at least 30 minutes, or up to 4 hours.

3 When you are ready to cook, heat a large griddle or frying pan over a high heat until a few drops of water 'dance' when they hit the surface. Use crumpled kitchen paper or a pastry brush to very lightly grease the hot pan with oil.

4 Use tongs to lift the prawns out of the marinade, letting the excess drip back into the bowl, then place the prawns on the griddle and leave them to cook for 2 minutes. Flip the prawns over and cook for a further 1–2 minutes until they turn pink, curl and are opaque all the way through when you cut one. Serve immediately.

prawn biryani

SERVES 8

1 tsp saffron strands

50 ml/2 fl oz tepid water

2 shallots, roughly chopped

3 garlic cloves, crushed

1 tsp chopped fresh ginger

2 tsp coriander seeds

½ tsp black peppercorns

2 cloves

seeds from 2 green
cardamom pods

½ cinnamon stick

1 tsp ground turmeric

1 fresh green chilli,
chopped

½ tsp salt

2 tbsp ghee

1 tsp black mustard seeds

500 g/1 lb 2 oz raw tiger
prawns, peeled and
deveined

300 ml/10 fl oz coconut
milk

300 ml/10 fl oz natural
yogurt

toasted flaked almonds,
to garnish

sliced spring onion,
to garnish

sprigs of fresh coriander,
to garnish

freshly cooked rice,
to serve

1 Soak the saffron in the tepid water for 10 minutes. Put the shallots, garlic, ginger, coriander seeds, peppercorns, cloves, cardamom seeds, cinnamon stick, turmeric, chilli and salt into a spice grinder or mortar and pestle and grind to a paste.

2 Heat the ghee in a saucepan and add the mustard seeds. When they start to pop, add the prawns and stir over a high heat for 1 minute. Stir in the spice mix, then the coconut milk and yogurt. Simmer for 20 minutes.

3 Spoon the prawn mixture into serving bowls. Top with the freshly cooked rice and drizzle over the saffron water. Serve garnished with the flaked almonds, spring onion and sprigs of coriander.

prawns with spinach

SERVES 4–6

150 ml/5 fl oz vegetable oil

½ tsp mustard seeds

½ tsp onion seeds

2 tomatoes, sliced

350 g/12 oz fresh spinach, roughly chopped

1 tsp finely chopped fresh ginger

1 garlic clove, crushed

1 tsp chilli powder

1 tsp salt

225 g/8 oz frozen prawns, defrosted and drained

1 Heat the oil in a large frying pan. Add the mustard and onion seeds to the frying pan.

2 Reduce the heat and add the tomatoes, spinach, ginger, garlic, chilli powder and salt to the frying pan and stir-fry for 5–7 minutes.

3 Drain the prawns thoroughly and add to the spinach mixture in the frying pan.

4 Stir the prawns into the spinach mixture until well blended, then cover and leave to simmer over a low heat for 7–10 minutes.

5 Spoon the mixture into a warmed serving dish and serve hot.

bengali prawns

SERVES 4

4 fresh green chillies, deseeded

4 spring onions, chopped

3 garlic cloves

2.5-cm/1-inch piece fresh ginger, chopped

2 tsp sunflower oil

4 tbsp mustard oil or vegetable oil

1 tbsp ground coriander

1 tsp mustard seeds, crushed

175 ml/6 fl oz coconut milk

500 g/1 lb 2 oz raw tiger prawns, peeled and deveined

115 g/4 oz chopped fresh coriander, plus extra leaves to garnish

salt

freshly cooked rice, to serve

lemon halves, to serve

1 Place the chillies, spring onions, garlic, ginger and sunflower oil in a food processor and process to a smooth paste. Heat the mustard oil in a large, heavy-based frying pan. Add the spice paste and cook over a low heat, stirring constantly, for 2 minutes.

2 Add the ground coriander, mustard seeds and coconut milk and bring to the boil, stirring constantly. Reduce the heat and simmer for 5 minutes.

3 Stir in the prawns and simmer for a further 6–8 minutes, or until they have just turned pink. Season with salt to taste, stir in the chopped coriander and serve immediately with freshly cooked rice and lemon halves. Garnish with a few coriander leaves.

prawn masala

SERVES 4

2 fresh red chillies, deseeded and chopped

2 garlic cloves, chopped

½ onion, chopped

2.5-cm/1-inch piece fresh ginger, chopped

1 tsp ground turmeric

1 tsp ground cumin

1 tsp garam masala

½ tsp sugar

½ tsp pepper

300 ml/10 fl oz natural yogurt

2 tbsp chopped fresh coriander

500 g/1 lb 2 oz raw tiger prawns, peeled, deveined and tails left intact

lime wedges, to serve

naan bread, to serve

1 If you are using wooden skewers, soak them in cold water for 30 minutes.

2 Put the chillies into a food processor with the garlic, onion, ginger, turmeric, cumin, garam masala, sugar, pepper and yogurt. Process until smooth, then transfer to a large, shallow dish. Stir in the coriander. Thread the prawns onto metal kebab skewers or pre-soaked wooden skewers, leaving a small space at either end. Transfer them to the dish and turn in the mixture until thoroughly coated. Cover with clingfilm and refrigerate for 1–1½ hours.

3 Preheat the grill. Remove from the refrigerator and arrange the skewers on a grill rack. Cook under a preheated medium grill, turning and basting with the marinade, for 4 minutes, until sizzling and cooked through.

4 Serve hot with naan bread and lime wedges for squeezing over.

prawn tikka with pineapple

MAKES 4

1 tsp cumin seeds

1 tsp coriander seeds

½ tsp fennel seeds

½ tsp yellow mustard seeds

¼ tsp fenugreek seeds

¼ tsp nigella seeds

pinch of chilli powder

pinch of salt

2 tbsp lemon or pineapple juice

12 raw tiger prawns, peeled, deveined and tails left intact

12 bite-sized wedges of fresh or well-drained canned pineapple

chopped fresh coriander, to garnish

1 If you are using wooden skewers, rather than metal ones, soak them in cold water for 30 minutes.

2 Dry-fry the cumin, coriander, fennel, mustard, fenugreek and nigella seeds in a hot frying pan over a high heat, stirring them around constantly, until you can smell the aroma of the spices. Immediately tip the spices out of the pan so they do not burn.

3 Put the spices in a spice grinder or mortar, add the chilli powder and salt and grind to a fine powder. Transfer to a non-metallic bowl and stir in the lemon juice.

4 Add the prawns to the bowl and stir them around so they are well coated, then set aside to marinate for 10 minutes. Meanwhile, preheat the grill to high.

5 Thread three prawns and three pineapple wedges alternately onto each metal or pre-soaked wooden skewer. Grill about 10 cm/4 inches from the heat for 2 minutes on each side, brushing with any leftover marinade, until the prawns turn pink and are cooked through.

6 Serve the prawns and pineapple wedges on a plate and garnish with coriander.

prawn & squid laksa

SERVES 4

225 g/8 oz dried rice noodles

2 tbsp vegetable oil

2 red chillies, deseeded and roughly chopped

700 ml/1¼ pints canned coconut milk

2 fish stock cubes

3 fresh kaffir lime leaves

2 tbsp red curry paste

1 bunch of spring onions, roughly chopped

225 g/8 oz raw squid, cleaned and cut into rings

225 g/8 oz large raw prawns, peeled and deveined

handful of fresh coriander, chopped, plus leaves to garnish

1 Soak the noodles in a saucepan of boiling water for 4 minutes, covered, until just tender, or according to the packet instructions. Drain, rinse under cold running water and set aside.

2 In a saucepan, heat the oil and fry the chillies for 1 minute. Add the coconut milk, stock cubes, lime leaves, curry paste and spring onions and bring gently to the boil, stirring occasionally. Reduce the heat and simmer, stirring occasionally, for 2–3 minutes until the stock cubes and paste have dissolved.

3 Add the squid and prawns and simmer for 1–2 minutes until the squid has plumped up and the prawns have turned pink. Add the cooked noodles and coriander and stir well. Serve immediately in soup bowls, garnished with coriander leaves.

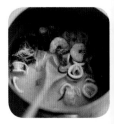

prawns in coconut milk

SERVES 4

4 onions

4 tbsp ghee or vegetable oil

1 tsp garam masala

1 tsp ground turmeric

1 cinnamon stick

2 cardamom pods, lightly crushed

½ tsp chilli powder

2 whole cloves

2 bay leaves

400 ml/14 fl oz coconut milk

1 tsp sugar

500 g/1 lb 2 oz raw tiger prawns, peeled and deveined

salt

freshly cooked pilau rice, to serve

1 Finely chop two of the onions and grate the other two. Heat the ghee in a large, heavy-based frying pan. Add the garam masala and cook over a low heat, stirring constantly, for 1 minute, or until its aroma is released. Add the chopped onions and cook, stirring occasionally, for 10 minutes, or until golden.

2 Stir in the grated onions, turmeric, cinnamon, cardamom pods, chilli powder, cloves and bay leaves and cook, stirring constantly, for 5 minutes. Stir in half the coconut milk and the sugar and season to taste with salt. Add the prawns and cook, stirring frequently for 8 minutes, or until they have just turned pink.

3 Stir in the remaining coconut milk and bring to the boil. Taste and adjust the seasoning, if necessary, and serve immediately with freshly cooked pilau rice.

prawns with curried noodles

SERVES 4

1 tbsp vegetable or groundnut oil

3 shallots, chopped

1 fresh red chilli, deseeded and chopped

1 tbsp red curry paste

1 lemon grass stalk (white part only), finely chopped

225 g/8 oz cooked prawns, peeled

400 g/14 oz canned straw mushrooms, drained

2 tbsp Thai fish sauce

2 tbsp Thai soy sauce

225 g/8 oz fresh egg noodles

chopped fresh coriander, to garnish

1 Heat the oil in a wok and stir-fry the shallots and chilli for 2–3 minutes. Add the curry paste and lemon grass and stir-fry for 2–3 minutes.

2 Add the prawns, mushrooms, fish sauce and soy sauce and stir well to mix.

3 Meanwhile, cook the noodles in boiling water for 3–4 minutes. Drain and transfer to warmed plates.

4 Top the noodles with the prawn curry, garnish with coriander and serve immediately.

goan prawn curry with eggs

SERVES 4

4 tbsp sunflower or olive oil

1 large onion, finely chopped

2 tsp ginger paste

2 tsp garlic paste

2 tsp ground coriander

½ tsp ground fennel

½ tsp ground turmeric

½–1 tsp chilli powder

½ tsp pepper

2–3 tbsp water

125 g/4½ oz canned chopped tomatoes

200 ml/7 fl oz coconut milk

1 tsp salt, or to taste

4 hard-boiled eggs

700 g/1 lb 9 oz cooked tiger prawns, peeled

juice of 1 lime

2–3 tbsp chopped fresh coriander leaves

freshly cooked basmati rice, to serve

1 Heat the oil in a medium saucepan over a medium–high heat and add the onion. Cook until the onion is softened but not browned. Add the ginger and garlic pastes and cook for 2–3 minutes.

2 In a small bowl, mix the ground coriander, ground fennel, turmeric, chilli powder and pepper. Add the water and make a paste. Reduce the heat to medium, add this paste to the onion mixture and cook for 1–2 minutes. Reduce the heat to low and continue to cook for 3–4 minutes.

3 Add half the tomatoes and cook for 2–3 minutes. Add the remaining tomatoes and cook for a further 2–3 minutes.

4 Add the coconut milk and salt, bring to a slow simmer and cook, uncovered, for 6–8 minutes, stirring regularly.

5 Meanwhile, shell the eggs and, using a sharp knife, make four slits lengthways on each egg without cutting them through. Add the eggs to the pan along with the prawns. Increase the heat slightly and cook for 6–8 minutes.

6 Stir in the lime juice and half the coriander. Remove from the heat and transfer the curry to a warmed serving dish. Garnish with the reserved coriander and serve with freshly cooked basmati rice.

prawns with spring onions & mushrooms

SERVES 4

2 tbsp vegetable or groundnut oil

1 bunch of spring onions, chopped

2 garlic cloves, finely chopped

175 g/6 oz creamed coconut, roughly chopped

2 tbsp red curry paste

450 ml/16 fl oz fish stock

2 tbsp Thai fish sauce

2 tbsp Thai soy sauce

6 sprigs of fresh Thai basil

400 g/14 oz canned straw mushrooms, drained

350 g/12 oz large cooked prawns, peeled

freshly cooked jasmine rice, to serve

1 Heat the oil in a wok and stir-fry the spring onions and garlic for 2–3 minutes. Add the creamed coconut, curry paste and stock and heat gently until the coconut has dissolved.

2 Stir in the fish sauce and soy sauce, then add the basil, mushrooms and prawns. Gradually bring to the boil and serve immediately with freshly cooked jasmine rice.

VARIATION

Replace the straw mushrooms with 300 g/10½ oz fresh shiitake mushrooms and add them to the pan with the spring onions.

Vibrant
Vegetables

tofu & vegetable curry

SERVES 4

vegetable or groundnut oil, for deep-frying

225 g/8 oz firm tofu, drained and cut into cubes

2 tbsp vegetable or groundnut oil

2 onions, chopped

2 garlic cloves, chopped

1 fresh red chilli, deseeded and sliced

3 celery sticks, diagonally sliced

225 g/8 oz mushrooms, thickly sliced

115 g/4 oz baby corn, cut in half

1 red pepper, deseeded and cut into strips

3 tbsp red curry paste

400 ml/14 fl oz coconut milk

1 tsp palm sugar or soft, light brown sugar

2 tbsp Thai soy sauce

225 g/8 oz baby spinach leaves

1 Heat the oil for deep-frying in a preheated wok or a deep saucepan or deep-fat fryer to 180–190°C/350–375°F, or until a cube of bread browns in 30 seconds. Add the tofu cubes, in batches, and cook for 4–5 minutes until crisp and brown all over. Remove with a slotted spoon, drain on kitchen paper and set aside.

2 Heat the 2 tablespoons of oil in a wok or frying pan and stir-fry the onions, garlic and chilli for 1–2 minutes, until they start to soften. Add the celery, mushrooms, corn and red pepper and stir-fry for 3–4 minutes, until they soften.

3 Stir in the curry paste and coconut milk and gradually bring to the boil. Add the sugar and soy sauce and then the spinach. Cook, stirring constantly, until the spinach has wilted. Serve immediately, topped with the tofu.

chickpea curry

SERVES 4

6 tbsp vegetable oil

2 onions, sliced

**1 tsp finely chopped fresh
ginger**

1 tsp ground cumin

1 tsp ground coriander

1 tsp crushed fresh garlic

1 tsp chilli powder

**2 fresh green chillies,
finely chopped**

**2–3 tbsp fresh coriander
leaves**

150 ml/5 fl oz water

1 large potato

**400 g/14 oz canned
chickpeas, drained**

1 tbsp lemon juice

1 Heat the oil in a large, heavy-based saucepan. Add the onions and cook, stirring occasionally, until golden. Reduce the heat, add the ginger, ground cumin, ground coriander, garlic, chilli powder, green chillies and coriander leaves and stir-fry for 2 minutes.

2 Add the water to the mixture in the saucepan and stir to mix.

3 Using a sharp knife, cut the potato into dice, then add with the chickpeas to the saucepan. Cover and leave to simmer, stirring occasionally, for 5–7 minutes.

4 Sprinkle the lemon juice over the curry. Transfer to warmed serving dishes and serve hot.

vegetable korma

SERVES 4

4 tbsp ghee or vegetable oil

2 onions, chopped

2 garlic cloves, chopped

1 fresh red chilli, chopped

1 tbsp grated fresh ginger

2 tomatoes, peeled and chopped

1 orange pepper, deseeded and cut into small pieces

1 large potato, cut into chunks

200 g/7 oz cauliflower florets

½ tsp salt

1 tsp ground turmeric

1 tsp ground cumin

1 tsp ground coriander

1 tsp garam masala

200 ml/7 fl oz vegetable stock or water

150 ml/5 fl oz natural yogurt

150 ml/5 fl oz single cream

25 g/1 oz fresh coriander, chopped

freshly cooked rice, to serve

1 Heat the ghee in a large saucepan over a medium heat. Add the onions and garlic and cook, stirring, for 3 minutes. Add the chilli and ginger and cook for a further 4 minutes.

2 Add the tomatoes, orange pepper, potato, cauliflower, salt and spices and cook, stirring, for a further 3 minutes. Stir in the stock and bring to the boil. Reduce the heat and simmer for 25 minutes.

3 Stir in the yogurt and cream and cook, stirring, for a further 5 minutes. Add the fresh coriander and heat through. Serve with freshly cooked rice.

kashmiri vegetables

SERVES 4

3 tbsp ghee or vegetable oil

2 tbsp flaked almonds

8 cardamom seeds

8 black peppercorns

2 tsp cumin seeds

1 cinnamon stick

2 fresh green chillies, deseeded and chopped

1 tsp ginger paste

1 tsp chilli powder

3 potatoes, cut into chunks

225 g/8 oz okra, cut into 2.5-cm/1-inch pieces

½ cauliflower, broken into florets

150 ml/5 fl oz natural yogurt

150 ml/5 fl oz vegetable stock or water

salt

freshly cooked rice, to serve

1 Heat 1 tablespoon of the ghee in a heavy-based saucepan. Add the almonds and cook over a low heat, stirring constantly, for 2 minutes, or until golden.

2 Remove the almonds from the saucepan with a slotted spoon, drain on kitchen paper and set aside. Place the cardamom seeds, peppercorns, cumin seeds and cinnamon stick in a spice grinder or mortar and grind finely.

3 Add the remaining ghee to the saucepan and heat. Add the green chillies and cook, stirring frequently, for 2 minutes. Stir in the ginger paste, chilli powder and ground spices and cook, stirring constantly, for 2 minutes, or until they give off their aroma.

4 Add the potatoes, season with salt to taste. Cover and cook, stirring occasionally, for 8 minutes. Add the okra and cauliflower and cook for a further 5 minutes.

5 Gradually stir in the yogurt and stock and bring to the boil. Cover and simmer for a further 10 minutes, until all the vegetables are tender. Garnish with the reserved flaked almonds and serve with freshly cooked rice.

cauliflower & sweet potato curry

SERVES 4

4 tbsp ghee or vegetable oil

2 onions, finely chopped

1 tsp panch phoran

1 cauliflower, broken into small florets

350 g/12 oz sweet potatoes, diced

2 fresh green chillies, deseeded and finely chopped

1 tsp ginger paste

2 tsp paprika

1½ tsp ground cumin

1 tsp ground turmeric

½ tsp chilli powder

3 tomatoes, quartered

225 g/8 oz fresh or frozen peas

3 tbsp natural yogurt

225 ml/8 fl oz vegetable stock or water

1 tsp garam masala

salt

sprigs of fresh coriander, to garnish

1 Heat the ghee in a large, heavy-based frying pan. Add the onions and panch phoran and cook over a low heat, stirring frequently, for 10 minutes, or until the onions are golden. Add the cauliflower, sweet potatoes and green chillies and cook, stirring frequently, for 3 minutes.

2 Stir in the ginger paste, paprika, cumin, turmeric and chilli powder and cook, stirring constantly, for 3 minutes. Add the tomatoes and peas and stir in the yogurt and stock. Season with salt to taste, cover and simmer for 20 minutes, or until the vegetables are tender.

3 Sprinkle the garam masala over the curry, transfer to a warmed serving dish and serve immediately, garnished with sprigs of fresh coriander.

chilli-yogurt mushrooms

SERVES 4–6

**55 g/2 oz ghee or 4 tbsp
vegetable or groundnut
oil**

2 large onions, chopped

**4 large garlic cloves,
crushed**

**400 g/14 oz canned
chopped tomatoes**

1 tsp ground turmeric

1 tsp garam masala

½ tsp chilli powder

**750 g/1 lb 10 oz chestnut
mushrooms, thickly
sliced**

pinch of sugar

**125 ml/4 fl oz natural
yogurt**

salt and pepper

**chopped fresh coriander,
to garnish**

**freshly cooked rice,
to serve**

1 Heat the ghee in a wok or large frying pan over a medium–high heat. Add the onions and cook, stirring frequently, for 5–8 minutes until golden. Stir in the garlic and cook for a further 2 minutes.

2 Add the tomatoes and mix around. Stir in the turmeric, garam masala and chilli powder and continue cooking for a further 3 minutes.

3 Add the mushrooms, sugar and salt to taste and cook for about 8 minutes, until the mushrooms have given off their liquid and are softened and tender.

4 Turn off the heat, then stir in the yogurt, a little at a time, beating vigorously to prevent it curdling. Taste and adjust the seasoning, adding salt and pepper if necessary. Garnish with coriander and serve with freshly cooked rice.

vegetable curry

SERVES 4

1 aubergine

225 g/8 oz turnips

350 g/12 oz new potatoes

225 g/8 oz cauliflower

**225 g/8 oz button
mushrooms**

1 large onion

3 carrots

6 tbsp ghee

2 garlic cloves, crushed

4 tsp chopped fresh ginger

**1–2 fresh green chillies,
deseeded and chopped**

1 tbsp paprika

2 tsp ground coriander

1 tbsp curry powder

**450 ml/16 fl oz vegetable
stock**

**400 g/14 oz canned
chopped tomatoes**

**1 green pepper, deseeded
and sliced**

1 tbsp cornflour

150 ml/5 fl oz coconut milk

2–3 tbsp ground almonds

salt and pepper

**sprigs of fresh coriander,
to garnish**

**freshly cooked rice,
to serve**

1 Cut the aubergine, turnips and potatoes into 1-cm/
½-inch cubes. Divide the cauliflower into small florets.
Leave the button mushrooms whole or slice them thickly, if
preferred. Slice the onion and carrots.

2 Heat the ghee in a large, heavy-based saucepan. Add the
onion, turnips, potatoes and cauliflower and cook over
a low heat, stirring frequently, for 3 minutes. Add the garlic,
ginger, chillies, paprika, ground coriander and curry powder
and cook, stirring, for 1 minute.

3 Add the stock, tomatoes, aubergine and mushrooms,
and season to taste with salt. Cover and simmer, stirring
occasionally, for 30 minutes, or until tender. Add the green
pepper and carrots, cover and cook for a further 5 minutes.

4 Place the cornflour and coconut milk in a bowl, mix into
a smooth paste and stir into the vegetable mixture. Add
the ground almonds and simmer, stirring constantly, for
2 minutes. Taste and adjust the seasoning, adding salt and
pepper if necessary. Transfer to warmed serving plates,
garnish with sprigs of coriander and serve immediately with
freshly cooked rice.

red curry with mixed leaves

SERVES 4

2 tbsp groundnut oil or vegetable oil

2 onions, thinly sliced

1 bunch of fine asparagus spears

400 ml/14 fl oz coconut milk

2 tbsp red curry paste

3 fresh kaffir lime leaves

225 g/8 oz baby spinach leaves

2 heads bok choi, chopped

1 small head Chinese leaves, shredded

handful of fresh coriander, chopped

freshly cooked rice, to serve

1 Heat a wok over a medium–high heat and add the oil. Add the onions and asparagus and stir-fry for 1–2 minutes.

2 Add the coconut milk, curry paste and lime leaves and bring gently to the boil, stirring occasionally.

3 Add the spinach, bok choi and Chinese leaves and cook, stirring, for 2–3 minutes, until wilted. Add the coriander and stir well. Serve immediately with freshly cooked rice.

carrot & pumpkin curry

SERVES 4

150 ml/5 fl oz vegetable stock

2.5-cm/1-inch piece fresh galangal, sliced

2 garlic cloves, chopped

1 lemon grass stalk (white part only), finely chopped

2 fresh red chillies, deseeded and chopped

4 carrots, cut into chunks

225 g/8 oz pumpkin, peeled, deseeded and cubed

2 tbsp vegetable or groundnut oil

2 shallots, finely chopped

3 tbsp yellow curry paste

400 ml/14 fl oz coconut milk

4–6 sprigs of fresh Thai basil

25 g/1 oz toasted pumpkin seeds, to garnish

1 Pour the stock into a large saucepan and bring to the boil. Add the galangal, half the garlic, the lemon grass and chillies and simmer for 5 minutes. Add the carrots and pumpkin and simmer for 5–6 minutes, until tender.

2 Meanwhile, heat the oil in a wok or frying pan and stir-fry the shallots and the remaining garlic for 2–3 minutes. Add the curry paste and stir-fry for 1–2 minutes.

3 Stir the shallot mixture into the saucepan and add the coconut milk and Thai basil. Simmer for 2–3 minutes. Serve hot and garnish with the toasted pumpkin seeds.

courgette &
cashew nut curry

SERVES 4

**2 tbsp vegetable or
groundnut oil**

6 spring onions, chopped

2 garlic cloves, chopped

**2 fresh green chillies,
deseeded and chopped**

**450 g/1 lb courgettes,
cut into thick slices**

**115 g/4 oz shiitake
mushrooms, halved**

55 g/2 oz beansprouts

**85 g/3 oz cashew nuts,
toasted or dry-fried**

**a few Chinese chives,
snipped**

4 tbsp Thai soy sauce

1 tsp Thai fish sauce

**freshly cooked noodles,
to serve**

1 Heat the oil in a wok or large frying pan and cook the spring onions, garlic and chillies for 1–2 minutes, until softened but not browned.

2 Add the courgettes and mushrooms and cook for 2–3 minutes until tender.

3 Add the beansprouts, cashew nuts, chives, soy sauce and fish sauce and stir-fry for 1–2 minutes. Serve hot with freshly cooked noodles.

green bean & potato curry

SERVES 6

300 ml/10 fl oz vegetable oil

1 tsp white cumin seeds

1 tsp mixed mustard and onion seeds

4 dried red chillies

3 tomatoes, sliced

1 tsp salt

1 tsp finely chopped fresh ginger

1 tsp crushed fresh garlic

1 tsp chilli powder

200 g/7 oz green beans, diagonally sliced into 2.5-cm/1-inch pieces

2 potatoes, diced

300 ml/10 fl oz water

chopped fresh coriander, to garnish

finely sliced green chillies, to garnish

1 Heat the oil in a large, heavy-based saucepan. Add the white cumin seeds, mustard and onion seeds and dried red chillies, stirring well.

2 Add the tomatoes to the pan and stir-fry the mixture for 3–5 minutes.

3 Mix the salt, ginger, garlic and chilli powder together in a bowl and spoon into the saucepan. Stir the whole mixture together.

4 Add the green beans and potatoes to the saucepan and stir-fry for 5 minutes.

5 Add the water to the saucepan, reduce the heat and simmer for 10–15 minutes, stirring occasionally. Transfer to a warmed serving dish, garnish with chopped coriander and green chillies and serve immediately.

thai vermicelli soup

SERVES 4

15 g/½ oz dried shiitake mushrooms

1.2 litres/2 pints vegetable stock

1 tbsp groundnut oil

4 spring onions, sliced

115 g/4 oz baby corn, sliced

2 garlic cloves, crushed

2 fresh kaffir lime leaves, chopped

2 tbsp red curry paste

85 g/3 oz rice vermicelli noodles

1 tbsp light soy sauce

2 tbsp chopped fresh coriander, to garnish

1. Place the mushrooms in a bowl, cover with the vegetable stock and leave to soak for 20 minutes.

2. Heat the groundnut oil in a saucepan over a medium heat. Add the spring onions, baby corn, garlic and kaffir lime leaves. Fry for 3 minutes to soften.

3. Add the red curry paste, soaked mushrooms and their soaking liquid. Bring to the boil and simmer for 5 minutes, stirring occasionally.

4. Add the noodles and soy sauce to the red curry mixture in the pan. Return the pan to the boil and simmer for a further 4 minutes until the noodles are just cooked. Garnish with the coriander and serve immediately.

potato & pepper curry

SERVES 4

3 tbsp ghee or vegetable oil

1 onion, chopped

2 potatoes, cut into large chunks

1 tsp chilli powder

1 tsp ground coriander

¼ tsp ground turmeric

2 green peppers, deseeded and cubed

225 g/8 oz fresh or frozen broad beans

200 g/7 oz canned tomatoes

2 fresh green chillies, roughly chopped

1 tbsp chopped fresh coriander

125 ml/4 fl oz vegetable stock or water

salt

naan bread, to serve

1 Heat the ghee in a large, heavy-based saucepan. Add the onion and cook over a low heat, stirring occasionally, for 5 minutes, or until softened. Add the potatoes and cook, stirring occasionally, for 5 minutes.

2 Add the chilli powder, ground coriander and turmeric and stir well. Then add the peppers, broad beans and the tomatoes and their can juices, breaking up the tomatoes slightly with a wooden spoon.

3 Stir in the green chillies and chopped coriander, pour in the stock and season to taste with salt. Cover and simmer for 8–10 minutes, or until the potatoes are tender. Serve immediately with naan bread.

egg & lentil curry

SERVES 4

3 tbsp ghee or vegetable oil

1 large onion, chopped

2 garlic cloves, chopped

2.5-cm/1-inch piece fresh ginger, chopped

½ tsp chilli powder

1 tsp ground coriander

1 tsp ground cumin

1 tsp paprika

85 g/3 oz split red lentils

450 ml/16 fl oz vegetable stock

225 g/8 oz canned chopped tomatoes

6 eggs

50 ml/2 fl oz coconut milk

2 tomatoes, cut into wedges

salt

sprigs of fresh coriander, to garnish

chapatis, to serve

1 Heat the ghee in a saucepan, add the onion and cook gently for 3 minutes. Stir in the garlic, ginger and spices and cook gently, stirring frequently, for 1 minute. Stir in the lentils, stock and tomatoes and bring to the boil. Reduce the heat, cover and simmer, stirring occasionally, for 30 minutes, until the lentils are tender.

2 Meanwhile, place the eggs in a saucepan of cold water and bring to the boil. Reduce the heat and simmer for 10 minutes. Drain and cover immediately with cold water.

3 Stir the coconut milk into the lentil mixture and season well with salt. Process the mixture in a blender or food processor until smooth. Return to the pan and heat through.

4 Shell the hard-boiled eggs and cut into quarters. Divide the hard-boiled egg quarters and tomato wedges between warmed serving plates. Spoon over the hot lentil sauce and garnish with sprigs of coriander. Serve hot with chapatis.

aubergine & bean curry

SERVES 4

2 tbsp vegetable or groundnut oil

1 onion, chopped

2 garlic cloves, crushed

2 fresh red chillies, deseeded and chopped

1 tbsp red curry paste

1 large aubergine, cut into chunks

115 g/4 oz pea or small aubergines

115 g/4 oz baby broad beans

115 g/4 oz fine French beans

300 ml/10 fl oz vegetable stock

55 g/2 oz creamed coconut, chopped

3 tbsp Thai soy sauce

1 tsp palm sugar or soft, light brown sugar

3 fresh kaffir lime leaves, roughly torn

4 tbsp chopped fresh coriander

1 Heat the oil in a wok or large frying pan and stir-fry the onion, garlic and chillies for 1–2 minutes. Stir in the curry paste and cook for 1–2 minutes.

2 Add the aubergines and cook for 3–4 minutes, until starting to soften. (You may need to add a little more oil as aubergines soak it up quickly.) Add all the beans and stir-fry for 2 minutes.

3 Pour in the stock and add the creamed coconut, soy sauce, sugar and lime leaves. Bring gently to the boil and simmer until the coconut has dissolved. Stir in the coriander and serve hot.

spicy chickpeas

SERVES 2–4

**400 g/14 oz canned
chickpeas, drained**

2 potatoes, diced

2 tbsp tamarind paste

6 tbsp water

1 tsp chilli powder

2 tsp sugar

1 onion, chopped

salt

**1 tomato, sliced,
to garnish**

**2 fresh green chillies,
chopped, to garnish**

**2–3 tbsp chopped fresh
coriander, to garnish**

1 Place the drained chickpeas in a large bowl.

2 Place the potatoes in a saucepan of water and boil until cooked through. Drain and set aside.

3 Mix the tamarind paste and water together in a small bowl.

4 Add the chilli powder, sugar and 1 teaspoon of salt to the tamarind paste mixture and mix together. Pour the mixture over the chickpeas.

5 Add the onion and the diced potatoes, and stir to mix. Season with a little salt to taste.

6 Transfer to a serving bowl and garnish with tomato, chillies and chopped coriander.

pumpkin curry

SERVES 4

150 ml/5 fl oz vegetable oil

2 onions, sliced

½ tsp white cumin seeds

450 g/1 lb pumpkin, peeled, deseeded and cubed

1 tsp aamchoor (dried mango powder)

1 tsp finely chopped fresh ginger

1 tsp crushed fresh garlic

1 tsp crushed fresh red chilli

½ tsp salt

300 ml/10 fl oz water

chapatis, to serve

1 Heat the oil in a large, heavy-based frying pan. Add the onions and cumin seeds and cook, stirring occasionally, for 5–6 minutes, until a light golden brown colour.

2 Add the pumpkin to the frying pan and stir-fry for 3–5 minutes over a low heat.

3 Mix the aamchoor, ginger, garlic, chilli and salt together in a bowl. Add to the onion and pumpkin mixture in the pan and stir well.

4 Add the water, cover and cook over a low heat for 10–15 minutes, stirring occasionally. Transfer the curry to warmed serving plates and serve hot with chapatis.

aubergine curry

SERVES 2

**groundnut or vegetable oil,
for deep-frying**

**2 aubergines, cut into
2-cm/¾-inch cubes**

**2 tbsp groundnut or
vegetable oil**

**1 bunch of spring onions,
roughly chopped**

2 garlic cloves, chopped

**2 red peppers, deseeded
and cut into 2-cm/¾-inch
squares**

3 courgettes, thickly sliced

**400 ml/14 fl oz coconut
milk**

2 tbsp red curry paste

**large handful of chopped
fresh coriander, plus
extra sprigs to garnish**

1 Heat the oil for deep-frying in a preheated wok, deep saucepan or deep-fat fryer to 180–190°C/350–375°F, or until a cube of bread browns in 30 seconds. Add the aubergine cubes, in batches, and cook for 45 seconds–1 minute until crisp and brown all over. Remove with a slotted spoon, drain on kitchen paper and set aside.

2 Heat the 2 tablespoons of oil in a separate preheated wok or large frying pan, add the spring onions and garlic and stir-fry over a medium–high heat for 1 minute. Add the red peppers and courgettes and stir-fry for 2–3 minutes. Add the coconut milk and curry paste and bring gently to the boil, stirring occasionally. Add the aubergines and chopped coriander, reduce the heat and simmer for 2–3 minutes.

3 Garnish with sprigs of coriander and serve immediately.

okra curry

SERVES 4

450 g/1 lb okra

150 ml/5 fl oz vegetable oil

2 onions, sliced

3 fresh green chillies, finely chopped

2 curry leaves

1 tsp salt

1 tomato, sliced

2 tbsp lemon juice

2 tbsp chopped fresh coriander

chapatis, to serve

1 Rinse the okra and drain thoroughly. Using a sharp knife, chop and discard the ends of the okra. Cut the okra into 2.5-cm/1-inch pieces.

2 Heat the oil in a large, heavy-based frying pan. Add the onions, chillies, curry leaves and salt and stir-fry for 5 minutes.

3 Gradually add the okra, mixing in gently with a slotted spoon, then stir-fry over a medium heat for 12–15 minutes.

4 Add the sliced tomato to the frying pan and sprinkle over the lemon juice sparingly.

5 Sprinkle with chopped coriander, cover and leave to simmer for 3–5 minutes. Transfer to warmed serving plates and serve hot with chapatis.

chinese greens curry

SERVES 4

2 tbsp vegetable or groundnut oil

1 fresh green chilli, deseeded and chopped

6 spring onions, sliced

3 tbsp green curry paste

115 g/4 oz bok choi

115 g/4 oz Chinese leaves

115 g/4 oz spinach

115 g/4 oz asparagus

3 celery sticks, sliced diagonally

3 tbsp Thai soy sauce

1 tsp palm sugar or soft, light brown sugar

juice of 1 lime

freshly cooked jasmine rice, to serve

1 Heat the oil in a wok or large frying pan and stir-fry the chilli and spring onions for 1–2 minutes. Add the curry paste and stir-fry for 2–3 minutes.

2 Add the bok choi, Chinese leaves, spinach, asparagus and celery and stir-fry for 3–4 minutes, until just tender.

3 Add the soy sauce, sugar and lime juice and cook for 30 seconds to heat through. Serve immediately with freshly cooked jasmine rice.

courgette curry

SERVES 4

6 tbsp vegetable oil

1 medium onion, finely chopped

3 fresh green chillies, finely chopped

1 tsp finely chopped fresh ginger

1 tsp crushed fresh garlic

1 tsp chilli powder

500 g/1 lb 2 oz courgettes, thinly sliced

2 tomatoes, sliced

2 tsp fenugreek seeds

chapatis, to serve

1 Heat the oil in a large, heavy-based frying pan. Add the onion, green chillies, ginger, garlic and chilli powder to the pan, stirring well to combine.

2 Add the courgettes and tomatoes to the pan and stir-fry over a medium heat, for 5–7 minutes.

3 Add the fenugreek seeds to the courgette mixture in the pan and stir-fry over a medium heat for a further 5 minutes, until the vegetables are tender.

4 Remove the pan from the heat and transfer to warmed serving dishes. Serve hot with chapatis.

butternut squash curry

SERVES 4

2 tbsp groundnut or vegetable oil

1 tsp cumin seeds

2 red onions, sliced

2 celery sticks, sliced

1 large butternut squash, peeled, deseeded and cut into chunks

2 tbsp green curry paste

300 ml/10 fl oz vegetable stock

2 fresh kaffir lime leaves

55 g/2 oz fresh beansprouts

handful of chopped fresh coriander, to garnish

freshly cooked rice, to serve

1 Heat the oil in a preheated wok, add the cumin seeds and stir-fry over a medium–high heat for 2–3 minutes until starting to pop.

2 Add the onions and celery and stir-fry for 2–3 minutes. Add the squash and stir-fry for 3–4 minutes. Add the curry paste, stock and lime leaves and bring to the boil, stirring occasionally.

3 Reduce the heat and simmer gently for 3–4 minutes until the squash is tender. Add the beansprouts and cook for a further 1–2 minutes until hot but still crunchy. Scatter the coriander over the curry and serve immediately with freshly cooked rice.

vegetable sambar

SERVES 6

**800 g/1 lb 12 oz canned
tomatoes**

2 tbsp desiccated coconut

2 tbsp lemon juice

**1 tbsp yellow mustard
seeds**

**40 g/1½ oz raw or
muscovado sugar**

2 tbsp ghee or vegetable oil

2 onions, sliced

**4 cardamom pods,
lightly crushed**

6 curry leaves

2 tsp ground coriander

2 tsp ground cumin

1 tsp ground turmeric

1 tsp ginger paste

200 g/7 oz toor dahl

**450 g/1 lb sweet potatoes,
cut into chunks**

**900 g/2 lb potatoes, cut into
chunks**

2 carrots, sliced

**2 courgettes, cut into
chunks**

**1 aubergine, cut into
chunks**

salt

1 Place the tomatoes and their can juices, the coconut, 1 tablespoon of the lemon juice, the mustard seeds and sugar in a food processor or blender and process until smooth.

2 Heat the ghee in a large, heavy-based saucepan. Add the onion and cook over a low heat, stirring occasionally, for 10 minutes, or until golden. Add the cardamom pods, curry leaves, coriander, cumin, turmeric and ginger paste and cook, stirring constantly, for 1–2 minutes, or until the spices give off their aroma.

3 Stir in the tomato mixture and dahl and bring to the boil. Reduce the heat, cover and simmer for 10 minutes.

4 Add the sweet potatoes, potatoes and carrots, re-cover the saucepan and simmer for a further 15 minutes. Add the courgettes, aubergine and remaining lemon juice, add salt to taste, re-cover and simmer for a further 10–15 minutes, or until the vegetables are tender.

chunky potato & spinach curry

SERVES 4

4 tomatoes

2 tbsp groundnut or vegetable oil

2 onions, cut into thick wedges

2.5-cm/1-inch piece fresh ginger, finely chopped

1 garlic clove, chopped

2 tbsp ground coriander

450 g/1 lb potatoes, cut into chunks

600 ml/1 pint vegetable stock

1 tbsp red curry paste

225 g/8 oz spinach leaves

1 Put the tomatoes in a heatproof bowl and cover with boiling water. Leave for 2–3 minutes, then plunge into cold water and peel off the skins. Cut each tomato into quarters and remove and discard the seeds and central core. Set aside.

2 Heat the oil in a preheated wok, add the onions, ginger and garlic and stir-fry over a medium–high heat for 2–3 minutes until starting to soften. Add the coriander and potatoes and stir-fry for 2–3 minutes. Add the stock and curry paste and bring to the boil, stirring occasionally. Reduce the heat and simmer gently for 10–15 minutes until the potatoes are tender.

3 Add the spinach and the tomato quarters and cook, stirring, for 1 minute, or until the spinach has wilted. Serve immediately.

VARIATION
Replace the potato chunks with the same amount of chopped sweet potato.

4

Appetizing
Accompaniments

coconut rice

SERVES 4–6

225 g/8 oz basmati rice

450 ml/16 fl oz water

60 g/2¼ oz creamed coconut

2 tbsp mustard oil

1½ tsp salt

toasted flaked coconut, to garnish

1 Rinse the basmati rice in several changes of water until the water runs clear, then leave to soak for 30 minutes. Drain and set aside until ready to cook.

2 Bring the water to the boil in a small saucepan, stir in the creamed coconut until it dissolves and then set aside.

3 Heat the mustard oil in a large frying pan or saucepan with a lid over a high heat until it smokes. Turn off the heat and leave the mustard oil to cool completely.

4 When you are ready to cook, reheat the mustard oil over a medium–high heat. Add the rice and stir until all the grains are coated in oil. Add the water with the dissolved coconut and bring to the boil.

5 Reduce the heat to as low as possible, stir in the salt and cover the pan tightly. Simmer, without lifting the lid, for 8–10 minutes until the grains are tender and all the liquid is absorbed.

6 Turn off the heat and use two forks to mix the rice. Re-cover the pan and leave the rice to stand for 5 minutes. Serve garnished with toasted flaked coconut.

pilau rice

SERVES 2–4

200 g/7 oz basmati rice

2 tbsp ghee

3 green cardamom pods

2 whole cloves

3 black peppercorns

½ tsp salt

½ tsp saffron threads

400 ml/14 fl oz water

1 Rinse the basmati rice in several changes of water until the water runs clear, then leave to soak for 30 minutes. Drain and set aside until ready to cook.

2 Heat a heavy-based saucepan over a medium–high heat, then add the ghee. Add the cardamom pods, cloves and peppercorns and stir-fry for 1 minute. Add the rice and stir-fry for a further 2 minutes.

3 Add the salt, saffron and water to the rice mixture and reduce the heat. Cover the pan and leave to simmer over a low heat for 20 minutes until the grains are tender and all the liquid is absorbed.

4 Transfer the rice to a large, warmed serving dish and serve hot.

lemon rice

SERVES 4–6

225 g/8 oz basmati rice

**25 g/1 oz ghee or 2 tbsp
vegetable or groundnut
oil**

1 tsp nigella seeds

450 ml/16 fl oz water

**finely grated rind and juice
of 1 large lemon**

1½ tsp salt

¼ tsp ground turmeric

1 Rinse the basmati rice in several changes of water until the water runs clear, then leave to soak for 30 minutes. Drain and set aside until ready to cook.

2 Heat the ghee in a large saucepan with a tight-fitting lid over a medium–high heat. Add the nigella seeds and rice and stir until all the grains are coated in ghee. Add the water and bring to the boil.

3 Reduce the heat to as low as possible, stir in half the lemon juice, the salt and turmeric and cover the pan tightly. Simmer, without lifting the lid, for 8–10 minutes until the grains are tender and all the liquid is absorbed.

4 Turn off the heat and use two forks to mix the lemon rind and remaining juice into the rice. Re-cover the pan and leave the rice to stand for 5 minutes before serving.

vegetable pakoras

SERVES 4

6 tbsp gram flour

½ tsp salt

1 tsp chilli powder

1 tsp baking powder

1½ tsp white cumin seeds

1 tsp pomegranate seeds

300 ml/10 fl oz water

¼ bunch of fresh coriander, finely chopped, plus extra sprigs to garnish

vegetables of your choice: cauliflower, cut into small florets; onions, cut into rings; potatoes, sliced; aubergines, sliced; or fresh spinach leaves

vegetable oil, for deep-frying

1 Sift the gram flour into a large bowl. Add the salt, chilli powder, baking powder, cumin and pomegranate seeds and blend together well. Pour in the water and beat well to form a smooth batter. Add the chopped coriander and mix well, then set aside.

2 Dip the prepared vegetables into the batter, carefully shaking off any excess.

3 Heat enough oil for deep-frying in a wok, deep-fat fryer or a large, heavy-based saucepan until it reaches 180°C/350°F, or until a cube of bread browns in 30 seconds. Using tongs, place the battered vegetables in the oil and deep-fry, in batches, turning once.

4 Repeat this process until all of the batter has been used up. Transfer the battered vegetables to crumpled kitchen paper and drain thoroughly. Garnish with coriander sprigs and serve immediately.

vegetable samosas

MAKES 8

1 carrot, diced

200 g/7 oz sweet potato, diced

85 g/3 oz frozen peas

2 tbsp ghee or vegetable oil

1 onion, chopped

1 garlic clove, chopped

2.5-cm/1-inch piece fresh ginger, grated

1 tsp ground turmeric

1 tsp ground cumin

½ tsp chilli powder

½ tsp garam masala

1 tsp lime juice

150 g/5½ oz plain flour, plus extra for dusting

3 tbsp butter, diced

4 tbsp warm milk

vegetable oil, for frying

salt and pepper

lime wedges, to serve

1 Bring a saucepan of water to the boil, add the carrot and cook for 4 minutes. Add the sweet potato and cook for 4 minutes, then add the peas and cook for a further 3 minutes. Drain and set aside.

2 Heat the ghee in a saucepan over a medium heat. Add the onion, garlic, ginger, spices and lime juice and cook, stirring, for 3 minutes. Add the vegetables and season to taste with salt and pepper. Cook, stirring, for 2 minutes. Remove from the heat and leave to cool for 15 minutes.

3 To make the pastry, put the flour into a bowl and rub in the butter. Add the milk and mix to form a dough. Knead briefly and divide into four pieces. On a lightly floured work surface, roll into balls, then roll out into circles 17 cm/6½ inches in diameter. Halve each circle, divide the filling between them and brush the edges with water, then fold over into triangles and seal the edges.

4 Heat 2.5 cm/1 inch of oil in a frying pan to 190°C/375°F, or until a cube of bread browns in 30 seconds. Using tongs, cook the samosas in batches for 3–4 minutes, or until golden. Drain on crumpled kitchen paper and serve hot with lime wedges.

onion bhajis

MAKES 12

**140 g/5 oz besan or gram
flour**

1 tsp salt

1 tsp ground cumin

1 tsp ground turmeric

1 tsp bicarbonate of soda

½ tsp chilli powder

2 tsp lemon juice

**2 tbsp vegetable or
groundnut oil, plus extra
for deep-frying**

2–8 tbsp water

2 onions, thinly sliced

**2 tsp coriander seeds,
lightly crushed**

1 Sift the besan flour, salt, cumin, turmeric, bicarbonate of soda and chilli powder into a large bowl. Add the lemon juice and the oil, then very gradually stir in just enough water until a batter, similar in consistency to single cream, forms. Mix in the onions and coriander seeds.

2 Heat enough oil for deep-frying in a wok, deep-fat fryer or large, heavy-based saucepan until it reaches 180°C/350°F, or until a cube of bread browns in 30 seconds. Without overcrowding the pan, drop in spoonfuls of the onion mixture and fry for 2 minutes, then use tongs to flip the bhajis over and continue frying for a further 2 minutes, or until golden brown.

3 Immediately remove the bhajis from the oil and drain well on crumpled kitchen paper. Keep the bhajis warm while you continue frying the remaining batter. Serve immediately.

plantain chips

SERVES 4

4 ripe plantains

1 tsp mild, medium or hot curry powder, to taste

vegetable or groundnut oil, for deep-frying

mango chutney, to serve

1 Peel the plantains, then cut crossways into 3-mm/⅛-inch slices. Put the slices in a bowl, sprinkle over the curry powder and use your hands to lightly toss together.

2 Heat enough oil for deep-frying in a wok, deep-fat fryer or large, heavy-based saucepan to 180°C/350°F, or until a cube of bread browns in 30 seconds. Add as many plantain slices as will fit in the pan without overcrowding and fry for 2 minutes, or until golden.

3 Remove the plantain chips from the pan with a slotted spoon and drain well on crumpled kitchen paper. Serve hot with mango chutney.

tamarind chutney

MAKES 250 G/9 OZ

100 g/3½ oz tamarind pulp, chopped

450 ml/16 fl oz water

½ fresh bird's eye chilli, or to taste, deseeded and chopped

55 g/2 oz soft light brown sugar, or to taste

½ tsp salt

1 Put the tamarind and water in a heavy-based saucepan over a high heat and bring to the boil. Reduce the heat to the lowest setting and simmer for 25 minutes, stirring occasionally to break up the tamarind pulp, or until tender.

2 Tip the tamarind pulp into a sieve and use a wooden spoon to push the pulp into the rinsed out pan.

3 Stir in the chilli, sugar and salt and continue simmering for a further 10 minutes or until the desired consistency is reached. Leave to cool slightly, then stir in extra sugar or salt, to taste.

4 Leave to cool completely, then transfer to an airtight container and chill for up to 3 days before using.

mango chutney

MAKES 250 G/9 OZ

**1 large mango, about
400 g/14 oz, peeled,
stoned and finely
chopped**

2 tbsp lime juice

**1 tbsp vegetable or
groundnut oil**

2 shallots, finely chopped

**1 garlic clove, finely
chopped**

**2 fresh green chillies,
deseeded and finely
sliced**

1 tsp black mustard seeds

1 tsp coriander seeds

**5 tbsp grated jaggery or
light brown sugar**

5 tbsp white wine vinegar

1 tsp salt

pinch of ground ginger

1 Put the mango in a non-metallic bowl with the lime juice and set aside.

2 Heat the oil in a large frying pan or saucepan over a medium–high heat. Add the shallots and cook for 3 minutes. Add the garlic and chillies and stir for a further 2 minutes, or until the shallots are softened, but not browned. Add the mustard and coriander seeds and then stir around.

3 Add the mango to the pan with the jaggery, vinegar, salt and ground ginger and stir around. Reduce the heat to its lowest setting and simmer for 10 minutes until the liquid thickens and the mango becomes sticky.

4 Remove from the heat and leave to cool completely. Transfer to an airtight container, cover and chill for 3 days before using. Store in the refrigerator and use within 1 week.

lime pickle

MAKES ABOUT 225 G/8 OZ

12 limes, halved and deseeded

115 g/4 oz salt

70 g/2½ oz chilli powder

25 g/1 oz mustard powder

25 g/1 oz ground fenugreek

1 tbsp ground turmeric

300 ml/10 fl oz mustard oil

15 g/½ oz yellow mustard seeds, crushed

½ tsp asafoetida

1 Cut each lime half into four pieces and pack them into a large sterilized jar, sprinkling over the salt at the same time. Cover and leave to stand in a warm place for 10–14 days, or until the limes have turned brown and softened.

2 Mix the chilli powder, mustard powder, fenugreek and turmeric together in a small bowl and add to the jar of limes. Stir to mix, then re-cover and leave to stand for 2 days.

3 Transfer the lime mixture to a heatproof bowl. Heat the mustard oil in a heavy-based frying pan.

4 Add the mustard seeds and asafoetida to the pan and cook, stirring constantly, until the oil is very hot and just beginning to smoke. Pour the oil and spices over the limes and mix well. Cover and leave to cool. When cool, pack into a sterilized jar, seal and store in a sunny place for 1 week before using.

chilli & onion chutney

MAKES ABOUT 225 G/8 OZ

1–2 fresh green chillies, deseeded or not, to taste, and finely chopped

1 small fresh bird's eye chilli, deseeded or not, to taste, and finely chopped

1 tbsp white wine vinegar or cider vinegar

2 onions, finely chopped

2 tbsp fresh lemon juice

1 tbsp sugar

3 tbsp chopped fresh coriander, mint or parsley, or a combination of herbs

salt

1 fresh red chilli flower, to garnish

1 To make the chilli flower garnish, use a sharp knife to make four cuts lengthways along the chilli. Place the point of the knife about 1 cm/½ inch from the stem end and cut towards the tip. Put the chilli in a bowl of iced water and let stand for 25–30 minutes, or until the cut edges have spread out to form a flower shape.

2 Put the green and bird's eye chillies in a small non-metallic bowl with the vinegar, stir around and then drain. Return the chillies to the bowl and stir in the onions, lemon juice, sugar and herbs, then add salt to taste.

3 Leave to stand at room temperature or cover and chill for 15 minutes. Garnish with the chilli flower before serving.

mung dahl

SERVES 4

225 g/8 oz mung beans or green lentils

3 tbsp vegetable oil

1 large onion, chopped

2 garlic cloves, crushed

2.5-cm/1-inch piece fresh ginger, grated

1 tsp ground turmeric

2 small fresh red chillies, deseeded and finely chopped

400 ml/14 fl oz cold water

2 tbsp desiccated coconut

1 tbsp cumin seeds

1 tsp black mustard seeds

salt and pepper

chapatis, to serve

1 Place the mung beans or lentils in a bowl and cover with water. Leave to soak for 3 hours or overnight, then drain.

2 Heat the oil in a large, heavy-based saucepan. Add the onion, garlic and ginger and fry over a medium heat for 5 minutes to soften.

3 Add the turmeric and chillies and fry for another minute.

4 Add the soaked mung beans or lentils and the cold water. Season to taste. Bring to the boil then reduce the heat and allow to simmer for 10 minutes or until the water is almost completely absorbed.

5 Meanwhile, place the coconut, cumin seeds and mustard seeds in a frying pan. Dry-fry for approximately 1 minute until the coconut is golden then stir into the cooked dahl. Serve hot with chapatis.

spiced basmati pilau

SERVES 4

500 g/1 lb 2 oz basmati rice

175 g/6 oz broccoli, trimmed

6 tbsp vegetable oil

2 large onions, chopped

225 g/8 oz mushrooms, sliced

2 garlic cloves, crushed

6 cardamom pods, split

6 whole cloves

8 black peppercorns

1 cinnamon stick or piece of cassia bark

1 tsp ground turmeric

1.2 litres/2 pints vegetable stock or water

55 g/2 oz seedless raisins

55 g/2 oz unsalted pistachios, roughly chopped

salt and pepper

1 Rinse the basmati rice in several changes of water until the water runs clear, then leave to soak for 30 minutes. Drain and set aside, until ready to cook. Trim off most of the broccoli stalk lengthways and cut diagonally into 1-cm/ ½-inch pieces.

2 Heat the oil in a large saucepan. Add the onions and broccoli stalks and cook over a low heat, stirring frequently, for 3 minutes. Add the mushrooms, rice, garlic and spices and cook for 1 minute, stirring, until the rice is coated in oil.

3 Add the stock and season to taste. Stir in the broccoli florets and return the mixture to the boil. Cover, reduce the heat and cook over a low heat for 15 minutes without uncovering the pan.

4 Remove the pan from the heat and leave the pilau to stand for 5 minutes without uncovering. Remove the whole spices, add the raisins and pistachios and gently fork through to fluff up the grains. Serve the pilau hot.

fruit & nut pilau

SERVES 4–6

225 g/8 oz basmati rice

450 ml/16 fl oz water

½ tsp saffron threads

1 tsp salt

25 g/1 oz ghee or 2 tbsp vegetable or groundnut oil

55 g/2 oz blanched almonds

1 onion, thinly sliced

1 cinnamon stick, broken in half

seeds from 4 green cardamom pods

1 tsp cumin seeds

1 tsp black peppercorns, lightly crushed

2 bay leaves

3 tbsp finely chopped dried mango

3 tbsp finely chopped dried apricots

2 tbsp sultanas

55 g/2 oz pistachio nuts, chopped

1 Rinse the basmati rice in several changes of water until the water runs clear, then leave to soak for 30 minutes. Drain and set aside until ready to cook.

2 Boil the water in a small saucepan. Add the saffron threads and salt, remove from the heat and set aside to infuse.

3 Heat the ghee in a large saucepan with a tight-fitting lid over a medium–high heat. Add the almonds and stir them around until golden brown, then immediately use a slotted spoon to scoop them out of the pan. Set aside.

4 Add the onion to the pan and cook, stirring frequently, for 5–8 minutes until golden, but not brown. Add the spices and bay leaves to the pan and stir them around for about 30 seconds.

5 Add the rice to the pan and stir until the grains are coated with ghee. Add the saffron-infused water and bring to the boil. Reduce the heat to as low as possible, stir in the dried fruit and cover the pan tightly. Simmer, without lifting the lid, for 8–10 minutes until the grains are tender and all the liquid is absorbed.

6 Turn off the heat and use two forks to mix the almonds and pistachios into the rice. Re-cover the pan and leave to stand for 5 minutes before serving.

coconut sambal

MAKES ABOUT 140 G/5 OZ

½ **fresh coconut or
125 g/4½ oz desiccated
coconut**

**2 fresh green chillies,
deseeded or not, to taste,
and chopped**

**2.5-cm/1-inch piece fresh
ginger, finely chopped**

**4 tbsp chopped fresh
coriander**

**2 tbsp lemon juice,
or to taste**

**2 shallots, very finely
chopped**

1 If you are using a whole coconut, use a hammer and nail to punch a hole in the 'eye' of the coconut, then pour out the water from the inside and reserve. Use the hammer to break the coconut in half, then peel half and chop.

2 Put the coconut and chillies in a food processor and process for about 30 seconds until finely chopped. Add the ginger, coriander and lemon juice and process again.

3 If the mixture seems too dry, stir in about 1 tablespoon of coconut water or water. Stir in the shallots and serve immediately, or cover and chill until required. This will keep its fresh flavour in the refrigerator for up to 3 days.

spicy lentil soup

SERVES 4

1 litre/1¾ pints water

250 g/9 oz toor dahl or chana dahl

1 tsp paprika

½ tsp chilli powder

½ tsp ground turmeric

2 tbsp ghee or vegetable oil

1 fresh green chilli, deseeded and finely chopped

1 tsp cumin seeds

3 curry leaves, roughly torn

1 tsp sugar

salt

1 tsp garam masala, to garnish

1 Bring the water to the boil in a large, heavy-based saucepan. Add the dahl, cover and simmer, stirring occasionally, for 25 minutes.

2 Stir in the paprika, chilli powder and turmeric, re-cover and cook for a further 10 minutes, or until the dahl is tender.

3 Meanwhile, heat the ghee in a small frying pan. Add the chilli, cumin seeds and curry leaves and cook, stirring constantly, for 1 minute.

4 Add the spice mixture to the dahl. Stir in the sugar and season to taste with salt. Ladle into warmed soup bowls, garnish with garam masala and serve immediately.

raita

SERVES 4–6

**1 large piece of cucumber,
about 300 g/10½ oz,
rinsed**

1 tsp salt

**400 ml/14 fl oz natural
yogurt**

½ tsp sugar

pinch of ground cumin

**2 tbsp chopped fresh
coriander or mint**

chilli powder, to garnish

1 Lay a clean tea towel flat on the work surface. Roughly grate the unpeeled cucumber directly onto the towel. Sprinkle with ½ teaspoon of the salt, then gather up the towel and squeeze until all the excess moisture is removed from the cucumber.

2 Put the yogurt into a bowl and beat in the remaining ½ teaspoon of salt, along with the sugar and cumin. Stir in the grated cucumber. Taste and add extra salt, if needed. Cover and chill until ready to serve.

3 Stir in the chopped coriander and transfer to a serving bowl. Sprinkle with chilli powder and serve.

naan bread

MAKES 10

900 g/2 lb strong white flour

1 tbsp baking powder

1 tsp sugar

1 tsp salt

300 ml/10 fl oz water, heated to 50°C/122°F

1 egg, beaten

55 g/2 oz ghee, melted, plus extra for rolling out and brushing

1 Sift the flour, baking powder, sugar and salt into a large mixing bowl and make a well in the centre. Mix together the water and egg, beating until the egg breaks up and is blended with the liquid. Slowly add the liquid mixture to the dry ingredients, using your fingers to draw in the flour from the sides, until a stiff, heavy dough forms. Shape the dough into a ball and return it to the bowl.

2 Cover the bowl with a damp tea towel, tucking the ends under the bowl. Set the bowl aside to let the dough rest for 30 minutes. Turn out the dough onto a work surface brushed with a little melted ghee and flatten the dough. Gradually sprinkle the dough with the melted ghee and knead to work it in, little by little, until it is completely incorporated. Shape the dough into 10 equal balls.

3 Resoak the towel in hot water and wring it out again, then place it over the dough balls and leave them to rest and rise for 1 hour. Meanwhile, put three baking sheets in the oven and preheat the oven to 230°C/450°F/Gas Mark 8 or its highest setting.

4 Use a lightly greased rolling pin to roll the dough balls into teardrop shapes, about 3 mm/⅛ inch thick. Use crumpled kitchen paper to lightly rub the hot baking sheets with ghee. Arrange the naans on the baking sheets and bake for 5–6 minutes until they are golden brown and lightly puffed. As you take the naans out of the oven, brush with melted ghee and serve immediately.

chapatis

MAKES 6

225 g/8 oz wholemeal flour, sifted, plus extra for dusting

½ tsp salt

150–200 ml/5–7 fl oz water

melted ghee, for brushing

1 Mix the flour and salt together in a large bowl and make a well in the centre. Gradually stir in enough of the water to make a stiff dough. Turn out the dough onto a lightly floured surface and knead for 10 minutes, or until it is smooth and elastic. Shape the dough into a ball and place it in the cleaned bowl, then cover with a damp tea towel and leave to rest for 20 minutes.

2 Divide the dough into six equal pieces. Lightly flour your hands and roll each piece of dough into a ball. Meanwhile, heat a large, ungreased, frying pan or griddle over a high heat until very hot and a splash of water 'dances' when it hits the surface.

3 Working with one ball of dough at a time, flatten the dough between your palms, then roll it out on a lightly floured work surface into an 18-cm/7-inch round. Slap the dough onto the hot pan and cook until brown flecks appear on the bottom. Flip the dough over and repeat on the other side.

4 Flip the dough over again and use a bunched-up tea towel to press down all around the edge. This pushes the steam in the chapati around, causing the chapati to puff up. Continue cooking until the bottom is golden brown, then flip over and repeat this step on the other side. Brush the chapati with melted ghee and serve, then repeat with the remaining dough balls. Chapatis are best served immediately, as soon as they come out of the pan, but they can be kept warm wrapped in foil for about 20 minutes.

spiced cashew nuts

SERVES 4

250 g/9 oz unsalted cashew nuts

1 tsp coriander seeds

1 tsp cumin seeds

2 green cardamom pods, crushed

1 tbsp sunflower oil

1 onion, thinly sliced

1 garlic clove, crushed

1 small fresh green chilli, deseeded and chopped

1 cinnamon stick

½ tsp ground turmeric

4 tbsp coconut cream

300 ml/10 fl oz vegetable stock

3 fresh kaffir lime leaves, finely shredded

freshly cooked jasmine rice, to serve

1 Soak the cashew nuts in cold water overnight. Drain thoroughly. Crush the coriander seeds, cumin seeds and cardamom pods to a fine powder using a pestle and mortar.

2 Heat the oil in a frying pan and stir-fry the onion and garlic for 2–3 minutes, or until softened but not browned. Add the chilli, crushed spices, cinnamon stick and turmeric and stir-fry for a further minute. Add the coconut cream and the hot stock to the pan.

3 Bring to the boil, then add the cashew nuts and lime leaves. Cover the pan, reduce the heat and simmer for 20 minutes. Serve hot with freshly cooked jasmine rice.

matar paneer

SERVES 4

**85 g/3 oz ghee or 6 tbsp
vegetable or groundnut
oil**

**350 g/12 oz paneer, cut into
1-cm/½-inch pieces**

**2 large garlic cloves,
chopped**

**1-cm/½-inch piece fresh
ginger, finely chopped**

1 large onion, finely sliced

1 tsp ground turmeric

1 tsp garam masala

¼–½ tsp chilli powder

**350 g/12 oz frozen peas
or 600 g/1 lb 5 oz fresh
peas, shelled**

1 fresh bay leaf

½ tsp salt

125 ml/4 fl oz water

**chopped fresh coriander,
to garnish**

1 Heat the ghee in a large frying pan or flameproof casserole with a tight-fitting lid over a medium–high heat. Add as many paneer pieces as will fit in a single layer without overcrowding the pan and cook for about 5 minutes until golden brown on all sides. Use a slotted spoon to remove the paneer and drain on crumpled kitchen paper. Continue, adding a little extra ghee, if necessary, until all the paneer is cooked.

2 Add the garlic, ginger and onion to the pan and cook, stirring frequently, for 5–8 minutes until the onion is softened, but not browned.

3 Stir in the turmeric, garam masala and chilli powder and cook for a further 2 minutes.

4 Add the peas, bay leaf and salt to the pan and stir around. Pour in the water and bring to the boil. Reduce the heat to very low, then cover and simmer for 10 minutes, or until the peas are tender.

5 Gently return the paneer to the pan. Simmer, stirring gently, until the paneer is heated through. Garnish with coriander and serve.

sag aloo

SERVES 4

**500 g/1 lb 2 oz fresh
spinach leaves**

2 tbsp ghee or vegetable oil

1 tsp black mustard seeds

1 onion, halved and sliced

**2 tsp garlic and ginger
paste**

**900 g/2 lb waxy potatoes,
cut into small chunks**

1 tsp chilli powder

**125 ml/4 fl oz vegetable
stock or water**

salt

1 Bring a large saucepan of water to the boil. Add the spinach leaves and blanch for 4 minutes. Drain well, then tip into a clean tea towel, roll up and squeeze out the excess liquid.

2 Heat the ghee in a separate saucepan. Add the mustard seeds and cook over a low heat, stirring constantly, for 2 minutes, or until they give off their aroma. Add the onion, and garlic and ginger paste and cook, stirring frequently, for 5 minutes, or until softened.

3 Add the potatoes, chilli powder and stock and season to taste with salt. Bring to the boil, cover and cook for 10 minutes. Add the spinach and stir it in, then cover and simmer for a further 10 minutes, or until the potatoes are tender. Serve immediately.

bombay potatoes

SERVES 6

500 g/1 lb 2 oz new potatoes, diced

1 tsp ground turmeric

pinch of salt

4 tbsp ghee or vegetable oil

6 curry leaves

1 dried red chilli

2 fresh green chillies, chopped

½ tsp nigella seeds

1 tsp mixed mustard and onion seeds

½ tsp cumin seeds

½ tsp fennel seeds

¼ tsp asafoetida

2 onions, chopped

5 tbsp chopped fresh coriander

juice of ½ lime

1 Place the potatoes in a large, heavy-based saucepan and pour in just enough cold water to cover. Add ½ teaspoon of the turmeric and the salt and bring to the boil. Simmer for 10 minutes, or until tender, then drain and set aside.

2 Heat a large, heavy-based frying pan over a medium–high heat, then add the ghee. Add the curry leaves and dried red chilli and cook, stirring frequently, for a few minutes, or until the chilli is blackened. Add the remaining turmeric, the green chillies, nigella seeds, mustard and onion seeds, cumin seeds, fennel seeds, asafoetida, onions and coriander and cook, stirring constantly, for 5 minutes, or until the onions have softened.

3 Add the potatoes, stir and cook over a low heat, stirring frequently, for 10 minutes, or until the potatoes have heated through. Squeeze over the lime juice and serve immediately.

aloo gobi

SERVES 4–6

55 g/2 oz ghee or 4 tbsp vegetable or groundnut oil

½ tbsp cumin seeds

1 onion, chopped

4-cm/1½-inch piece fresh ginger, finely chopped

1 fresh green chilli, deseeded and thinly sliced

450 g/1 lb cauliflower, cut into small florets

450 g/1 lb large waxy potatoes, cut into large chunks

½ tsp ground coriander

½ tsp garam masala

¼ tsp salt

sprigs of fresh coriander, to garnish

1 Heat the ghee in a flameproof casserole or large frying pan with a tight-fitting lid over a medium–high heat. Add the cumin seeds and stir around for about 30 seconds until they crackle and start to brown.

2 Immediately add the onion, ginger and chilli and stir for 5–8 minutes until the onion is golden.

3 Stir in the cauliflower and potato, followed by the ground coriander, garam masala and salt, and continue stirring for about 30 seconds longer.

4 Cover the pan, reduce the heat to the lowest setting and simmer, stirring occasionally, for 20–30 minutes until the vegetables are tender when pierced with the point of a knife. Check occasionally that they aren't sticking to the base of the pan and stir in a little water, if necessary.

5 Serve garnished with sprigs of coriander.

VARIATION
Replace the potatoes with the same weight of pumpkin or butternut squash, peeled and cut into chunks.